# ISRAEL AND THE GREAT COMMISSION

## HOW THE GREAT COMMISSION FULFILLS GOD'S PURPOSE FOR ISRAEL AND THE NATIONS

SAMUEL WHITEFIELD

ONE
KING
PUBLISHING

*Israel and the Great Commission—How the Great Commission Fulfills God's Purpose for Israel and the Nations*
By Samuel Whitefield

Published by OneKing Publishing
PO Box 375
Grandview, MO 64030

Email: contact@oneking.global
Web: https://oneking.global

Second Edition

ISBN: 978-1-7323380-2-9
eBook ISBN: 978-1-7323380-3-6

Dedicated to all who labor in obscurity to make the Lamb known to Israel and the nations.

*And now the Lord says, he who formed me from the womb to be his servant, to bring Jacob back to him; and that Israel might be gathered to him—for I am honored in the eyes of the Lord, and my God has become my strength—he says: "It is too light a thing that you should be my servant to raise up the tribes of Jacob and to bring back the preserved of Israel; I will make you as a light for the nations, that my salvation may reach to the end of the earth."* (Isaiah 49:5–6)

# Contents

# INTRODUCING ISRAEL AND THE GREAT COMMISSION

## How Does Israel Relate to the Great Commission?

The phrase *Great Commission* is the term we use most often to describe the assignment God has given the church in this age. It's a term that comes from the words of Jesus:

> *Go therefore and make disciples of all nations, baptizing them in the name of the Father and of the Son and of the Holy Spirit, teaching them to observe all that I have commanded you. And behold, I am with you always, to the end of the age. (Matthew 28:19–20)*

While there is much more to the church than the Great Commission, it is a concise summary of the church's assignment in this age. When most people think of the Great Commission, they think primarily of evangelizing the nations, but the task includes much more.

For the last two thousand years, the church has been struggling with how Gentile followers of Jesus should relate to Israel. Through much of church history, believers assumed God was finished with any unique destiny for the Jewish people and had transferred her promises to the church. For centuries, most of the church thought this was a settled issue, but the twentieth century changed all that.

For nearly two thousand years, Israel's story seemed finished, and then a madman started a world war and made his success in that war dependent on the annihilation of the Jewish people. The sudden reemergence of the State of Israel—something that defied all odds—immediately followed his gruesome attempt at genocide. Within the space of a decade, the world was suddenly forced to deal with the Holocaust and the establishment of the modern State of Israel. From 1948 to today, the nations continue to wrestle with the question of

Israel, and second to the person of Jesus, Israel has become perhaps the most polarizing issue in the earth.

The issue of Israel has especially challenged the church. One part of the church sees Israel as a relic of the past that is no longer significant to God's redemptive plan. Another part of the church sees a unique ongoing purpose for Israel in God's redemptive plan and sees deep, biblical significance in the events of the twentieth century. *Israel is vigorously discussed and debated in the church, but rarely discussed in the context of the Great Commission.*

However, if Israel is significant and if the Great Commission is the church's primary assignment in this age, we must view the question of Israel through the lens of the Great Commission to understand the state properly. Many believers see the Great Commission as a New Testament assignment that shifts the focus of the church away from Israel's story to the nations. Part of God's redemptive plan is to fulfill His promises to Israel because Israel and the nations are deeply connected in the context of the Great Commission. The command to go to the nations of the earth is not a new mission. It is the continuation of a mission that began in the Old Testament—a mission that is for the sake of Israel *and* the nations.

The purpose of this book is to understand Israel and the nations in the context of the Great Commission by examining the connections between key Old and New Testament passages. As we examine these passages, we will see the Great Commission was in God's heart from the beginning because it advances His purposes for Israel and the nations.

We do not have the space to examine in detail many of the passages and biblical themes referenced in this book. I would encourage readers to take advantage of other resources that further develop the passages and biblical concepts mentioned in this book.

We will discover the Great Commission has its roots in the Old Testament. It is not a new command but part of the progression of God's redemptive work. In the same way, Israel's story does not end with the Old Testament. It is an ongoing story that depends on the nations to come to fulfillment.

## An Unprecedented Moment in Church History

Before this age can come to an end, the gospel must be preached to every people group on the earth.[1] The church has labored for nearly two thousand years to fulfill this mission, and we are living in the first generation in human history where it is possible.[2] A tremendous amount of work remains to be done, but we are living in an unprecedented moment in church history. It has tremendous implications for how we understand the task of the church in our generation. As significant as this moment is, the evangelization of every people group is only one component of the Great Commission. To fully grasp the task of the church in this age, we need to understand the entire scope of the gospel mission.

The subject of the Great Commission and missions is not just about evangelism. Evangelism is only one aspect of missions. Missions exists to disciple the nations, and the core of discipleship is teaching the nations to observe all that Jesus commanded:

> *Go therefore and make disciples of all nations, baptizing them in the name of the Father and of the Son and of the Holy Spirit, teaching them to observe all that I have commanded you. And behold, I am with you always, to the end of the age. (Matthew 28:19–20)*

Missions is ultimately intended to prepare the earth for the return of Jesus, and the task is not complete until everything is accomplished that must happen before Jesus comes.

When we look at the Scriptures, there are two key signs that occur in the earth before the return of Jesus:

1.  There must be a saved remnant in every tribe and tongue.[3]

---

[1]  See Matthew 24:14; 28:19; Acts 1:8; Revelation 5:9; 7:9.

[2] While there is an acceleration in the preaching of the gospel, we must recognize that an enormous number of people have not yet heard it and many of the remaining people groups will be the most difficult to reach. The number of unreached people groups is decreasing, but the total number of people who still need a gospel witness numbers in the billions.

[3] See Matthew 24:14; 28:19; Acts 1:6–8; Revelation 5:9; 7:9.

2. A global controversy will erupt over the city of Jerusalem[4] and the salvation of all Israel.[5]

*We live in the first generation in human history where these two signs could potentially be fulfilled.* For centuries, the church has engaged in missions, but we are the first generation that has the potential to evangelize every people group. One hundred years ago, we did not even know where every people group in the earth was located, but now we have the possibility of seeing each people group receive a witness of the gospel. This is truly unprecedented.

At the same time, we are the first generation in over two thousand years to have a sovereign State of Israel setting the context for a global controversy. Furthermore, we are the first generation in human history with a global controversy around the city of Jerusalem. Never have all the nations of the earth been connected to the global controversy over Jerusalem.

If only one of these signs were happening in our generation, it would be significant. Both signs occurring in our generation at the same time demands our attention. We need to understand how these two signs are related, how the Bible says both will come to resolution, and what the role of the church is in their resolution to grasp all that is included in the Great Commission.

People tend to focus on Israel in the Old Testament and the nations in the New Testament, but a careful study of the Scripture reveals that Israel and the nations are woven together in the plan of God by the Great Commission. From the beginning in the Old Testament, the Bible makes promises to Israel and the nations; however, the Old Testament never explains completely how all these promises will be fulfilled. When we come to the New Testament, the Great Commission does not shift the storyline away from Israel to the nations; on the contrary, it brings together God's promises to Israel and the nations.

The Great Commission is not solely a command to go to the nations. It is the glue that binds together the promises to Israel and the

---

[4] See Isaiah 34; Joel 3; Zechariah 14; Matthew 24:15; Revelation 11.

[5] See Jeremiah 31:31–34; Ezekiel 36:27–36; Zechariah 12:10–12; Matthew 23:39; 24:30; Acts 1:6–7; Romans 11:26–27; Revelation 1:7.

promises to the nations. The commission is the way God is going to fulfill His promises. The church has tended to treat Israel and the Great Commission as two unrelated subjects when they are part of a single mission in God's heart. When we recognize this, we can better see the unity of God's plan and the role the church plays in it to fulfill His promises to Israel and the nations.

## Learning from History

To understand the confusion that currently exists related to the Great Commission—specifically the lack of understanding of Israel's ongoing election—we need to understand two components of church history. The first is the fall of Jerusalem in AD 70, and the second is the influence of a system of theology called Dispensationalism.

In AD 70, Rome concluded a long siege on Jerusalem by destroying the city. This was followed by almost a century of war during which Rome drove the majority of the Jewish population out of the region. Within a few centuries, the church became predominantly Gentile and the church began to assume that the destruction of Jerusalem in AD 70 and the subsequent diaspora of the Jewish people from the land were part of a final divine judgment on Israel. When Israel fell to Babylon in 586 BC, a Jewish remnant returned to the land approximately seventy years later. However, after Rome's destruction of Jerusalem, there was no immediate restoration of Israel. As the centuries unfolded, it seemed increasingly impossible that Israel would ever exist again, and therefore, most of the church adopted the assumption that God was finished with Israel.

The fall of Jerusalem in AD 70 influenced Christian theology far more than most of us recognize. To many theologians, it was the proof that God was finished with Israel. However, the sudden reemergence of the modern State of Israel in 1948 has been a profound challenge to the church's understanding of Israel. The twentieth century was marked by an attempted extermination of the Jewish people and the establishment of the modern State of Israel. Suddenly, Israel was in the center of the world stage, and as a result, the church is being forced to reexamine how it views the church and Israel.

The second component that profoundly affected the church's view of Israel is the prominence of Dispensationalism over the last one hundred years. Dispensationalism is a theological system developed in the nineteenth century that spread rapidly. It became so prominent that support for Israel is usually associated with Dispensationalism. It emphasized God had a future purpose for Israel but also separated His plan for the church from His plan for Israel.

When it first emerged, Dispensationalism basically proposed two peoples of God with two different plans of redemption. One was the church, and the other was Israel. As a result of this idea of "two peoples of God," Dispensationalism created a context for people to support Israel but see it as separate from the Gentile church and, therefore, separate from the Great Commission.

Due to Dispensationalism and other factors, the church's approach to Israel has often been more political than missional. *To many Christians, the question of Israel is primarily a political question* (i.e., do we support Israel's government?) *when it should be primarily a missional question* (do we recognize Israel's role in the plan of God and, therefore, cooperate with His plan to bring the gospel to her?). In the New Testament, the subject of Israel is primarily a missional one, and we need to restore that emphasis.[6] This does not make political issues unimportant, but the missional issues must be the priority.

Over time Dispensational theologians have proposed ways of correcting the error of two different people of God, but the effects of historical Dispensationalism are still being felt. To avoid this error, we must see the subject of Israel in the context of the Great Commission and the glorious plan of God to produce one people of God—both Jew and Gentile—brought together under Jesus.

## Israel and Unreached People Groups

Unreached people groups are those people groups either with no indigenous believers or a believing community that is so small it needs outside help from the global church to spread the gospel among its own people. A people group is considered reached when the church in that people group is large enough to be self-sustaining and self-expanding among that people group. The commission to the church to labor for the gospel among unreached people groups has profound implications for how we view Israel.

---

6 See Romans 1:16; 9:1–3.

While the establishment of a modern State of Israel was profoundly significant, Israel remains an unsaved nation. It is in deep need of the gospel. The regathering of a people and the founding of a nation are not enough to fulfill the promises of God. The promises of God are only available in Jesus,[7] and therefore, Israel's future is directly connected to Israel's King.

While there is a vibrant church in Israel, the nation remains statistically an unreached nation. This is shocking because most unreached people groups are in places that are difficult to reach with very little access to the gospel. Israel, on the other hand, hosts millions of Christian visitors and tourists each year, all the while remaining an unreached nation.

Obedience to the Great Commission means the global church should prioritize the nation of Israel as an unreached nation and support the gospel in that nation. However, Israel tends to be neglected in the conversation about world missions. It is time for that to shift. Biblically, Israel remains a priority in the Great Commission. As the apostle Paul declared:

> *For I am not ashamed of the gospel, for it is the power of God for salvation to everyone who believes, to the Jew first and also to the Greek. (Romans 1:16)*

---

[7] See John 14:6; Romans 6:23; 2 Corinthians 1:20; Galatians 3:22; 1 John 5:11.

# THE KNOWLEDGE OF GOD IN THE STORY OF ISRAEL

## God's Burning Desire to Reveal Himself

One of the great accusations against God is that He is distant, thus making it difficult to perceive who He is or what He wants. However, the issue is not God's distance but the dullness of the human heart as the result of sin. Not only is God not distant, He is also not silent. He is actively speaking in different ways.

The primary way He has spoken and continues to speak is through His Son:

> *Long ago, at many times and in many ways, God spoke to our fathers by the prophets, but in these last days he has spoken to us by his Son, whom he appointed the heir of all things, through whom also he created the world. (Hebrews 1:1–2)*

> *The words and life of Jesus are God's primary method of communicating His nature and His redemptive plan.*

Another way God speaks to the nations is through His Word. The Scriptures have been supernaturally recorded and preserved for us as the Word of God so that we can know and understand God:[1]

> *All Scripture is breathed out by God and profitable for teaching, for reproof, for correction, and for training in righteousness. (2 Timothy 3:16)*

A third way God speaks to us is through the nations and specifically through the story of Israel. God reveals Himself primarily through what He does and in the context of relationship. This explains

---

[1] See Psalm 19:7–11; 119:97–104, 130; Romans 15:4; 1 Corinthians 10:11; 2 Peter 1:19.

why the Bible is composed mostly of stories and not primarily of lists of God's attributes. The Bible defines God's attributes, but God reveals the full meaning of those attributes through His interactions with humanity. For example, God describes Himself as merciful, but He reveals His mercy through His interactions with men like David, Peter, and Paul.

God is a brilliant teacher, and He has formed the earth as an immersive classroom to instruct the nations in the knowledge of Himself. Everything we encounter is intended to instruct us—if we perceive it—in the knowledge of who God is and who man is:[2]

> *For what can be known about God is plain to them, because God has shown it to them. For his invisible attributes, namely, his eternal power and divine nature, have been clearly perceived, ever since the creation of the world, in the things that have been made. (Romans 1:19–20)*

God is not distant. He has a burning desire to reveal Himself, and He designed His interaction with Israel and the nations to reveal who He is. Israel in particular is a gift of God to the nations to instruct us in the knowledge of who God is and who man is. Therefore, we study Israel to better understand the knowledge of God.

## Israel's Story Is Ultimately about Israel's God

The story of Israel sets a context for God to glorify His Son. If we make Israel the primary point of the Bible, we will get off track, but if we keep Jesus central in Israel's story, we will avoid a number of errors and receive the full benefit of Israel's role in the redemptive story.

Israel's story is ultimately about Israel's God, and His glory is at stake in her story:

> *"Therefore say to the house of Israel, Thus says the Lord God: It is not for your sake, O house of Israel, that I am about to act, but for the sake of my holy name." (Ezekiel 36:22)*

If we do not perceive Israel correctly, we do not perceive who God is, because what happens with Israel instructs us about God. As Paul reflected on the story of Israel, it caused him to erupt in worship as he

---

2 See Psalm 19:1-6.

perceived the knowledge of God through Israel's story, and we want to do the same:

> *Oh, the depth of the riches and wisdom and knowledge of God! How unsearchable are his judgments and how inscrutable his ways! For who has known the mind of the Lord, or who has been his counselor? (Romans 11:33–34 ESV)*

## The Story of Israel Is a Presentation of the Gospel

Israel is God's parable to the earth, and through the story of Israel, God is instructing the nations. Not only does Israel's story reveal who God is, it also reveals who we are. Israel's story is intended by God to serve as a mirror for the rest of humanity. When we look at Israel's story, we are looking at our story. Israel reveals who we are, and God's interactions with Israel reveal His interactions with us.

This is why it is so critical we understand Israel's story and how her story ends. It is a flesh-and-blood presentation of the core issues of man's dilemma and God's plan to resolve man's crisis and deliver creation.

## The Story of Israel as a Summary of the Gospel

When we compare the story of Israel to the story of humankind, it becomes apparent that the story of Israel is God's summary of the plan of redemption.

It began at creation. When God created the earth, He created a number of creatures. He then chose one creature—man—among all the creatures on Earth and gave man the knowledge of God and the assignment to spread the knowledge of God to creation. *When God created the nations, He chose one nation—Israel—and revealed Himself to Israel in a unique way. He then commissioned Israel to display the knowledge of God to the nations.*

When God chose man, He did not choose man based on his qualifications, but chose man on the basis of His desire. God created man because He wanted him, not because He needed him. This is one of the profound truths of the gospel: Our relationship with God is based on His desire, not our attractiveness. Because God chose man for His purposes, God ultimately bears the responsibility of fulfilling man's purpose. *God chose Israel according to His own desire. Israel was the least of all people, and yet God set His love and affection on her.*[3] *Because God chose Israel on the basis of His choice and not her strength or ability, He bears the responsibility for bringing Israel into her calling.*

God made man in His own image,[4] and man served as the representation of God in the earth. *The tabernacle, and later the temple, given to Israel was a representation of God's presence on the earth. Israel's worship sanctuary was made as an earthy representation of what is in heaven.*[5]

Man was given a priestly calling and a land. Man was placed in the place of God's presence in the earth, and his life in "the land" (the garden) was intended to cause the presence of God to spread into the earth as man subdued the earth for God's purposes. *Israel was given a priestly calling and placed in a land. Israel was the only nation with a temple to the true God and was put among the nations to cultivate the presence of God. Her faithfulness in her land was intended to spread the knowledge of God into the nations.*

Man was given a simple, straightforward set of restrictions, but another creature in the garden—the serpent—seduced man, and he rebelled against God. As a result of that sin, man was driven from the garden and the presence of God. *Israel was given a simple set of rules but instead rebelled against God. Just as the serpent seduced man, the nations surrounding Israel seduced her into sin. As a result, Israel was driven from the land, and the divine presence and the temple was removed.*

When he seduced mankind, the enemy thought he had destroyed God's plan because God's agreement with man was sin would result in death. Man's disobedience did result in death, but God made a promise to save man. *In the same way, the enemy thought he had destroyed Israel when Israel fell into sin because the terms of the Mosaic Covenant resulted in the death of the nation if Israel violated the covenant.*

God did not replace humanity because man was not chosen on the basis of his own ability but on the basis of God's desire. Instead, God set into motion a plan to redeem humanity. To save mankind, God inserted Himself into humanity and became a man. Man had been sentenced to death, but God set into motion a plan to bring

---

[3] See Deuteronomy 7:7-8.

[4] See Genesis 1:27.

[5] See Hebrews 8:5.

resurrection. *When Israel sinned, God did not replace Israel because He did not choose her on the basis of her performance. Instead, He set into motion a process to save Israel. Israel's sin resulted in death for the nation, but God promised to restore the nation. Because of the terms of the covenant, God needed a perfect Israelite to save Israel, so God committed to become an Israelite. He inserted Himself into Israel to save her.*

God's honor is at stake in His ability to save humanity. If the enemy can destroy man through sin, then he has triumphed over God. However, if God can save humanity and accomplish His original intention, He triumphs over His enemy. The tragedy of man's story is that millions of humans will be lost, but God will bring about a day of salvation. Through God's redemptive effort, man will be saved. *God's honor is at stake in saving Israel. This is why Moses interceded for Israel's future on the basis of God's character.[6] Israel cannot be lost because God has the power to save. Tragically, millions of Israelites will be lost, but a day will come when Israel will be saved.*

God's plan to save humanity will save more than humanity. It will end up redeeming the cosmos. *God's plan to save Israel will do more than save Israel. It will also release salvation into the nations.*

## Israel's Story Is the Gospel

When we compare the plan of redemption to the story of Israel, we can see the story of Israel is the gospel. God is acting out His redemptive plan in the sight of all the nations to teach and instruct us. When we carefully consider Israel's story, it reveals the nature of God, the nature of man, and the nature of His salvation.

*Because the story of Israel is a presentation of the gospel, it is important how it ends.* Israel's story cannot simply end with the failure of Israel. It must end with Israel's salvation, just as the story of man cannot end with the fall. It must end in salvation.

## The Gospel Is at Stake in Israel's Story

When we consider Israel's story, we find that God is more tender and more severe than we can imagine. In His relationship with Israel, God reveals His love, His discipline, His judgments, His mercy, and His salvation. In His dealings with this people, God exposes who He is in

---

[6] See Exodus 32:11-13.

such an intimate way that He compares His relationship with Israel to a marriage.[7] *Therefore, what we think about Israel's story reflects what we think about God.* When we do not perceive Israel correctly, we miss something about who God is.

In the same way, the story of Israel is also the revelation of the knowledge of man. When we look at Israel, we are looking into a mirror. Her rebellion is our rebellion. Her redemption is our redemption. Israel's story gives us insight into humanity. We are called to be priests. We are rebellious. God has given us promises. We need a deliverer. We will be saved through a costly process. Israel instructs us in who we are.

God chose Israel on the basis of His desire and not her performance. Because Israel was not called by God not the basis of her performance, neither is she rejected by God on the basis of her failure. All of this shows us Israel's story is more than Israel's story—it is the telling of the gospel in an allegorical form.

If Israel illustrates man's failure, then Israel must also become a demonstration of man's redemption because when God called Israel He called Israel as a failure. She was the "least of all people" chosen entirely on the basis of God's desire and His ability to save.

If Israel's story ends with her rebellion, then God was not strong enough to redeem her, and her story was decided by her ability to perform rather than by God's ability to save. This is why it is so serious that Israel's story does not end with Israel's sin. *The gospel is at stake in Israel's story.*

---

[7] See Jeremiah 2:2; Ezekiel 16:8; Hosea 2:5-7.

# Israel and the Nations in the Old Testament

## The Great Commission and the Old Testament

Most believers assume the Old Testament is primarily about Israel and the New Testament primarily about the nations. There is no question the Old Testament focuses on Israel's story and the New Testament emphasizes God's gracious offer of mercy to the Gentiles and all that is entailed in it. However, the Old and New Testaments contain a single, unified story, with the Great Commission having deep roots in both Testaments. To fully understand the Great Commission, we have to deal with wrong assumptions. One of these is that the Great Commission is a New Testament idea. *The truth is, though, the roots of the Great Commission are in the Old Testament.*

## The Nations Were Born in Judgment but Destined for Redemption

The book of Genesis introduces the story of God's work in the nations. Genesis tells us how God created a beautiful world with incredible potential and how the fall of man threatened everything God intended for creation. In the early chapters of Genesis, we see crisis after crisis because of man's rebellion. The acceleration of wickedness in the earth was so rapid God found it necessary to send a cataclysmic flood to destroy the majority of humanity simply to slow the acceleration of darkness in the earth.

As traumatic as the flood was, it was not enough to stop man's rebellion. Not long after the flood, people conspired again to reject God and His leadership. They gathered together to build what we call the *Tower of Babel*. They said,

*"Come, let us build ourselves a city and a tower with its top in the heavens, and let us make a name for ourselves, lest we be dispersed over the face of the whole earth." And the Lord came down to see the city and the tower, which the children of man had built. And the Lord said, "Behold, they are one people, and they have all one language, and this is only the beginning of what they will do. And nothing that they propose to do will now be impossible for them. Come, let us go down and there confuse their language, so that they may not understand one another's speech." So the Lord dispersed them from there over the face of all the earth, and they left off building the city. Therefore its name was called Babel, because there the Lord confused the language of all the earth. And from there the Lord dispersed them over the face of all the earth. (Genesis 11:4–9)*

According to Genesis 11:4, one of the reasons men came together to build the tower was to prevent humankind from being dispersed over the face of the earth. It seems to be rebellion against the command God gave after the flood in Genesis 9:1 to be fruitful and fill the earth. God commanded man to fill the earth because He already had Revelation 5:9 and 7:9 in His heart:

*And they sang a new song, saying, "Worthy are you to take the scroll and to open its seals, for you were slain, and by your blood you ransomed people for God from every tribe and language and people and nation." (Revelation 5:9)*

*After this I looked, and behold, a great multitude that no one could number, from every nation, from all tribes and peoples and languages, standing before the throne and before the Lamb, clothed in white robes, with palm branches in their hands. (7:9)*

The building of the Tower of Babel was a direct challenge to God's sovereignty over man and God's desire to fill the earth with nations and people groups. Because man refused God's command to fill the earth, He divided humanity by giving them different languages. That division began the separation of mankind into different nations, cultures, languages, and people groups. Man refused to obey God's instructions, so God advanced His purpose for the nations with His judgment. *God's judgments are more than punishment. They also advance His redemptive purposes.* They are not vindictive; they are merciful.

The people groups of the earth began in judgment, but they will end in salvation. God's judgment at the Tower of Babel resulted in profound division among the people of the earth, but His plan of redemption is going to result in profound unity among the people of the earth. Judgment will end in redemption. Division will end in unity. *The diversity that began in judgment will produce a unified people in the earth according to God's original design.*

If we understand the nature of God and His judgments, when we read Genesis 11, we are left with two burning questions:

1.  How is God going to redeem the nations?

2.  How is God going to resolve this division of humanity so that it ends up being a glorious part of His redemptive plan?

## God Answers the Crisis through Election

In Genesis 12, God begins His process of redeeming the nations by choosing Abraham and giving him tremendous promises that will shape the rest of redemptive history. Those promises include specific promises for Abraham's descendants, but those promises are not just given for Abraham's sake. *God's covenant with Abraham in Genesis 12 is not a promise to save only one people group out of the nations; it is a promise to save a people group for the sake of the nations.*

> *Now the Lord said to Abram, "Go from your country and your kindred and your father's house to the land that I will show you. And I will make of you a great nation, and I will bless you and make your name great, so that you will be a blessing. I will bless those who bless you, and him who dishonors you I will curse, and in you all the families of the earth shall be blessed." (Genesis 12:1–3)*

God chose Abraham and his family as part of His plan to resolve the crisis of the fall and redeem the judgment of Genesis 11. It may seem odd to us that God would choose one person and his family for the sake of the world, but this is God's way. The Bible calls this *election.* Election occurs when God chooses a specific individual, or a specific people, and uses the person or specific people in a unique way to bring blessing to a larger group.

To understand God's purpose in election, we must begin by understanding two key principles of God's election. The first principle of election is: *God chooses people and nations according to His own sovereign will.* His choosing is not based on our ability, potential, or personal achievement because there is nothing "better" in any of us that causes us to deserve to be chosen by God. Because He does not choose the way we do, He frequently chooses people we would not choose. Consequently, His election of an individual, or a nation, often causes controversy and division. Jacob, Moses, David, Paul, Peter, and many others were unexpected and shocking choices. Israel rebelled against Moses. David's family did not even invite him when Samuel came to anoint a king from Jesse's sons because they never imagined David could be king.

The second principle of God's election is: *God chooses an individual for the benefit of the whole.* When we think of someone being chosen for a special purpose, we typically think of the honor it brings to the person who is chosen. God's choosing is different. Biblically, being chosen is ultimately for the sake of others, not for the sake of the person who was chosen. The priests of Israel are an example. They were not chosen because they were superior to the rest of Israel. They were anointed to perform a special function that would benefit the entire nation. God emphasized this point by forming the priesthood from a family line. The priests were not selected according to a process to determine who the most powerful or gifted people were. They were simply part of a family line chosen by God for a work that would bless the entire nation.

Jesus is the ultimate example of God's election. God chose to bring salvation by choosing one man and through that one man blessing would come to many. God's choice of Jesus was unexpected and controversial. God did not choose the man we would have chosen:

> *He had no form or majesty that we should look at him, and no beauty that we should desire him. He was despised and rejected by men, a man of sorrows and acquainted with grief; and as one from whom men hide their faces he was despised, and we esteemed him not. (Isaiah 53:2–3)*

God is the God who elects. He is the God who chooses. He continues to lead the church this way by anointing individuals in specific ways for the good of the entire body. We must understand

God's election so that we do not resist it or become offended by it. God told Abraham He would bless those who blessed him and curse those who cursed him:

> *I will bless those who bless you, and him who dishonors you I will curse, and in you all the families of the earth shall be blessed. (Genesis 12:3)*

God's election is controversial. Some agree with it and bless. Others disagree with it and curse. God's statement to Abraham is a warning of the controversy of His election and an instruction to us that we can receive great blessing when we agree with His election.

There are many challenges associated with God's election. One challenge is the one who is chosen can assume he is more important and use his election for his own benefit or privilege. Philippians 2 addresses this issue by calling us to have the same thinking as Jesus, who used His privilege for the benefit of others. If Jesus—the one man born worthy of His calling—used His election for the sake of others, how much more should we use any privilege God gives us for the sake of others?

> *Have this mind among yourselves, which is yours in Christ Jesus, who, though he was in the form of God, did not count equality with God a thing to be grasped, but emptied himself, by taking the form of a servant, being born in the likeness of men. And being found in human form, he humbled himself by becoming obedient to the point of death, even death on a cross. (Philippians 2:5–8)*

Another challenge is people can become offended because they interpret God's election as a statement God values that person more than He does the rest. This can also lead to intense envy towards a person who is chosen or uniquely anointed by God. This offense usually manifests in finding fault with those God has chosen to "prove" that they should not have been chosen and, therefore, are insufficient for the task. *The ones God chooses for a special task are always insufficient for the task, because they were not chosen based on their own ability.*

God chooses according to His own purposes. We must recognize none of us deserves any special privilege, and what privileges we may receive are ultimately for the sake of others. Understanding God's plan of election is the key to understanding Genesis 12.

In Genesis 12, God elects a specific man and a specific people for a unique redemptive purpose, and that election is for the good of all. So, Genesis 12 is the beginning of a plan to not just save Israel but to save the nations. God makes this plain by telling Abraham His plan for Abraham's family will bring blessing to all the families of the earth —"people groups" in modern language.

> *Now the Lord said to Abram, "Go from your country and your kindred and your father's house to the land that I will show you. And I will make of you a great nation, and I will bless you and make your name great, so that you will be a blessing. I will bless those who bless you, and him who dishonors you I will curse, and in you all the families of the earth shall be blessed." (Genesis 12:1–3)*

## God Remains Committed to Election

Israel failed to serve the nations because of her own sin, her lack of revelation of her calling to serve the nations, and the rage of the nations. The nations failed to recognize God's call on Israel because of their rage against Him, their lack of understanding of what He was doing, and their resulting envy. *However, God remains committed to accomplishing His purposes through election.*

Israel's obedience was never the basis of her calling, and therefore, her disobedience—though it has serious consequences—does not invalidate her calling.

> *As regards the gospel, they are enemies for your sake. But as regards election, they are beloved for the sake of their forefathers. For the gifts and the calling of God are irrevocable. For just as you were at one time disobedient to God but now have received mercy because of their disobedience, so they too have now been disobedient in order that by the mercy shown to you they also may now receive mercy. For God has consigned all to disobedience, that he may have mercy on all. (Romans 11:28–32)*

The gifts and callings—the election of God—are irrevocable. He calls people and nations for redemptive purposes. When the nations sin, it has serious implications, but it does not invalidate the calling. We see that with nations and with individuals. To fully understand God's redemptive plan, we must recognize how committed God is to accomplish His purposes through election.

## Three Key Promises

When God made covenant with Abraham, He gave him three key promises:

1.  God promised a specific land to Abraham.
2.  God promised Abraham his descendants would become a great nation and make his name great in the earth.
3.  God promised what happens with Abraham through His family will bring great blessing to all the families of the earth.

All three of these promises are tightly bound together. God cannot fulfill just one of these promises; He must fulfill all three. As the redemptive story unfolds, we see how tightly connected these promises are.

Galatians refers to God's promise to Abraham as a prediction that the nations would be included in God's family. According to Paul, when God gave Abraham His promises, He was preaching the gospel to him. In a sense, Abraham was the first one to be given the essence of what would become the Great Commission.

> *And the Scripture, foreseeing that God would justify the Gentiles by faith, preached the gospel beforehand to Abraham, saying, "In you shall all the nations be blessed." (Galatians 3:8)*

These promises made to Abraham were ultimately made to Jesus. God chose Jesus to fulfill Abraham's promises because Jesus alone can fulfill them.

> *Now the promises were made to Abraham and to his offspring. It does not say, "And to offsprings," referring to many, but referring to one, "And to your offspring," who is Christ. (Galatians 3:16)*

Many assume that, because Abraham's promises were promises given to Jesus, they are somehow changed in the New Testament. This is a radical theological leap Paul never makes. Paul does not say Abraham's promises should be reinterpreted. He says God is fully committed to fulfilling His promises to Israel and the nations through His Son, Jesus.

As the Old Testament unfolded, it built on these promises. For example, when God called Jacob, He gave Jacob the same exact promise He had given to Abraham.

> *And behold, the Lord stood above it and said, "I am the Lord, the God of Abraham your father and the God of Isaac. The land on which you lie I will give to you and to your offspring. Your offspring shall be like the dust of the earth, and you shall spread abroad to the west and to the east and to the north and to the south, and in you and your offspring shall all the families of the earth be blessed." (Genesis 28:13–14)*

*These promises were never fulfilled during Abraham's or Jacob's lifetimes.* Both lived like strangers in the land. Neither saw their descendants become a great and mighty people, nor did they see all the people groups of the earth come into blessing. These three key promises have never been fulfilled in history, but God will fulfill them before the end of the age. The Great Commission will play a role in their fulfillment.

## Joseph—A Picture of God's Plan for Israel and the Nations

The story of Joseph is one of the most profound prophecies of God's redemptive plan. Joseph's mother could not conceive until God miraculously opened her womb.[1] Joseph was the favorite son of his father.[2] Not only was Joseph his father's favorite, he was also given dreams that he would become the most prominent member in his family. His brothers, father, and mother would all bow down to him one day.[3]

Joseph's trouble began when he was sent by his father to find his brothers who were shepherds.[4] Joseph found his brothers, but they rejected him and sold him as a slave to the Gentiles.[5] After being sold as a slave, Joseph faithfully served the Gentiles in Egypt, and ultimately was given tremendous power and authority as Pharaoh's second in

---

[1] See Genesis 30:22-24.

[2] See Genesis 37:4.

[3] See Genesis 37:5-11.

[4] See Genesis 37:13-17.

[5] See Genesis 37:18-28.

command. Joseph was thirty years old when he stood before Pharaoh and began his public service in Egypt.[6]

Joseph married an Egyptian woman,[7] and he prepared Egypt for a seven-year famine.[8] During that famine, Joseph's family was forced to go to Egypt for grain to survive.[9] Because Joseph had preserved Egypt's food supply, he was able to feed his family. Sadly, when his brothers first came to Egypt, they did not recognize him. Even though they did not know his true identity, he continued to provide for them until the day he revealed himself to them. When that happened, there was great weeping as the family was emotionally reunited. When he was restored to his family, Joseph recognized his rejection and his labor in Egypt were part of a God-ordained plan to save Egypt and the family of Israel.[10]

Joseph's life illustrates how God uses His unique plan of election to fulfill His promises. Joseph was chosen from among His brothers for special honor. His brothers responded in envy, but because God chose Joseph, the entire family was saved. In many ways, the life of Joseph is a prophecy of Jesus' labor in the nations. This is apparent when we compare Jesus' life to Joseph's.

Jesus' birth was supernatural.[11] Mary could not have conceived apart from a miracle. Jesus was the favorite Son of His Father.[12] Jesus was born to be Israel's greatest Son, and one day the entire family of Israel—even the patriarchs Abraham, Isaac, and Jacob—will bow down to Him.[13] Jesus was sent to find the lost sheep of Israel.[14] Jesus likely began His public ministry around the age of thirty. Though many in

---

[6] See Genesis 41:46.

[7] See Genesis 41:45.

[8] See Genesis 41:33-36.

[9] See Genesis 42:1-2.

[10] See Genesis 45:5-9.

[11] See Luke 1:26-38.

[12] See Matthew 3:17; 17:5; Mark 1:11; 9:7; Luke 3:22; 9:35; 2 Peter 1:17.

[13] See Isaiah 9:6; Daniel 7:13-14; Luke 24:52; John 5:23; 8:53-58; 9:35-38; Colossians 1:17; Hebrews 1:6; 3:3; Revelation 1:11, 17; 5:9-14.

[14] See Matthew 15:24.

Israel followed Jesus, the nations as a whole rejected Him and He was sold for a price.[15]

The rejection of Jesus by Israel resulted in the gospel being carried to the Gentiles.[16] While Jesus has never abandoned the Jewish people and there has always been a saved Jewish remnant, there is a sense in which Jesus has become a Servant among the Gentiles for nearly two thousand years. Like Joseph, Jesus has taken a Gentile bride from the nations and joined Himself to her.

Just as Joseph's labor in Egypt ultimately served a purpose to save His family, so also Jesus' labor among the nations is going to serve His purpose of restoring Israel to relationship with Him. Joseph used the harvest of Egypt to make provision for Israel. In the same way, Jesus' harvest among the Gentiles is going to make provision for Israel during a coming seven-year tribulation. The famine Egypt faced should have been devastating, but instead Joseph shrewdly used the famine to purchase all of Egypt for Pharaoh. In the same way, Jesus is going to use the end of the age to bring everything under His ownership so He can ultimately hand it over to the Father.[17]

Zechariah's prophecy of the day when Israel's eyes are opened to see Jesus as her Deliverer should be read with the story of Joseph's restoration to his brothers in mind:

*"And I will pour out on the house of David and the inhabitants of Jerusalem a spirit of grace and pleas for mercy, so that, when they look on me, on him whom they have pierced, they shall mourn for him, as one mourns for an only child, and weep bitterly over him, as one weeps over a firstborn. On that day the mourning in Jerusalem will be as great as the mourning for Hadad-rimmon in the plain of Megiddo. The land shall mourn, each family by itself: the family of the house of David by itself, and their wives by themselves; the family of the house of Nathan by itself, and their wives by themselves. (Zechariah 12:10–12)*

---

[15] See Matthew 23:37; 26:14-16; John 1:11; 19:15, 21.

[16] See Romans 11:11.

[17] See 1 Corinthians 15:24.

When Hosea predicts that Israel will seek God's face in her distress, he is ultimately referring to Jesus' face, and he also has the story of Joseph in mind:

*I will return again to my place, until they acknowledge their guilt and seek my face, and in their distress earnestly seek me. (Hosea 5:15)*

Joseph's story is unique, but it is not the only biblical picture of God's plan to bring together Israel and the Gentiles. Throughout Israel's history, there were individuals, like Rahab and Ruth, who were Gentiles but became a key part of Israel's story. Some even became part of the Messiah's family line. *These individuals were a prophetic statement that God is going to bring the Gentiles and the Jewish people together into one family.*

## The Great Commission's Old Testament Foundations

God's covenant with Abraham sets the stage for the Great Commission. Throughout the Old Testament, there are prophetic pictures of the Great Commission in biblical characters like Joseph, Rahab, Ruth, and others. The Old Testament prophets also predicted God's intention for the nations:

*"As for me, I have set my King on Zion, my holy hill." I will tell of the decree: The Lord said to me, "You are my Son; today I have begotten you. Ask of me, and I will make the nations your heritage, and the ends of the earth your possession." (Psalm 2:6–8)*

*All the ends of the earth shall remember and turn to the Lord, and all the families of the nations shall worship before you. For kingship belongs to the Lord, and he rules over the nations. (22:27–28)*

*They lift up their voices, they sing for joy; over the majesty of the Lord they shout from the west. Therefore in the east give glory to the Lord; in the coastlands of the sea, give glory to the name of the Lord, the God of Israel. From the ends of the earth we hear songs of praise, of glory to the Righteous One. But I say, "I waste away, I waste away. Woe is me! For the traitors have betrayed, with betrayal the traitors have betrayed." (Isaiah 24:14–16)*

*Sing to the Lord a new song, his praise from the end of the earth, you who go down to the sea, and all that fills it, the coastlands and their inhabitants. Let the desert and its cities lift up their voice, the villages that Kedar inhabits; let the habitants of Sela sing for joy, let them shout from the top of the mountains. Let them give glory to the Lord, and declare his praise in the coastlands. (42:10–12)*

*And now the Lord says, he who formed me from the womb to be his servant, to bring Jacob back to him; and that Israel might be gathered to him—for I am honored in the eyes of the Lord, and my God has become my strength—he says: "It is too light a thing that you should be my servant to raise up the tribes of Jacob and to bring back the preserved of Israel; I will make you as a light for the nations, that my salvation may reach to the end of the earth." (49:5–6)*

*Sing and rejoice, O daughter of Zion, for behold, I come and I will dwell in your midst, declares the Lord. And many nations shall join themselves to the Lord in that day, and shall be my people. And I will dwell in your midst, and you shall know that the Lord of hosts has sent me to you. (Zechariah 2:10–11)*

*Then everyone who survives of all the nations that have come against Jerusalem shall go up year after year to worship the King, the Lord of hosts, and to keep the Feast of Booths. (14:16)*

*For from the rising of the sun to its setting my name will be great among the nations, and in every place incense will be offered to my name, and a pure offering. For my name will be great among the nations, says the Lord of hosts. (Malachi 1:11)*

The Old Testament tells Israel's story, but it is more than Israel's story. It is also the story of God's plan to save the nations through His plan with Israel. He elected Israel for a specific purpose, which is why the Old Testament predominantly tells Israel's story, but that election is for the sake of the nations. When we look at the Old Testament through this lens, we see it consistently pointing towards God's story with Israel bringing salvation to the nations. From the beginning, God desired the nations and wanted an inheritance from every people group.

Because God works through the plan of election, He picks one nation for the sake of the other nations. When we do not understand election properly, we view the Old Testament as Israel's story and the

New Testament as the story of the nations. In reality, the Old Testament is the story of Israel and the nations. Israel's election set into motion the Great Commission. However, there is more to the story, and the Great Commission is going to end with the nations honoring Israel's election by tenderly calling her back to her God.

# THE NEW TESTAMENT, ISRAEL, AND THE NATIONS

## Is the New Testament the End of Israel's Story?

The idea that the Great Commission is solely a New Testament idea is one wrong assumption that must be corrected. There is another assumption we must also address: The New Testament's emphasis on the nations discards any unique redemptive purpose for Israel. The Great Commission commands the church to disciple the nations, but to fully obey it we must remember the command is given in the context of a redemptive story. This story joins together the salvation of Israel with the salvation of the nations.

We have been commissioned to bring the nations into obedience to all of Jesus' teaching, so we must examine what Jesus said about Israel and the nations. If we read the Great Commission in Matthew 28 without any context, it can seem as though the Great Commission is solely focused on the nations. However, if we look carefully at a few New Testament passages, we can see Israel's story continues in the New Testament.

## Matthew 21

Matthew 21–24 tells the story of Jesus' entering Jerusalem as King, His rejection by the religious leaders, the disciples' confusion, and Jesus' commitment to fulfill everything the prophets predicted. Throughout these chapters, Jesus emphasized His commitment to Israel and the nations. In Matthew 21, Jesus rebuked the religious leaders and reminded them the temple was to be known as a place of prayer:

> He said to them, "It is written, 'My house shall be called a house of prayer,' but you make it a den of robbers." (Matthew 21:13)

To fully understand Jesus' rebuke, we have to recognize it is a quotation from Isaiah 56:7:

*"These I will bring to my holy mountain, and make them joyful in my house of prayer; their burnt offerings and their sacrifices will be accepted on my altar; for my house shall be called a house of prayer for all peoples."*

Isaiah prophesied that the temple was to become a house of prayer for all people. When Jesus cleansed the temple and gave His rebuke, He addressed two issues:

1. Israel must come into her calling. The nation is called to demonstrate pure worship and to be known as a place of prayer.

2. Israel's calling is ultimately to be a place of prayer for the nations. Jesus was reminding Israel of her call to the nations and God's intention to invite the nations into His house.

## Matthew 23

Matthew recorded some of Jesus' harshest rebukes in chapter 23, but he ended the chapter with Jesus' tender words about Jerusalem:

*O Jerusalem, Jerusalem, the city that kills the prophets and stones those who are sent to it! How often would I have gathered your children together as a hen gathers her brood under her wings, and you were not willing! (v. 37)*

Matthew 23:37 is an amazing look at Jesus' heart towards Jerusalem. He described Jerusalem as the city who kills the prophets, but instead of following that statement with a sentence of judgment, He described His deep desire to protect, preserve, and care for the city. Despite Jerusalem's rebellion, Jesus' primary desire was to gather, protect, preserve, and nurture the city. Because the Father is going to give Jesus whatever He asks for,[1] this verse hints that a day is coming when Jerusalem will come under Jesus' leadership and He will be able to gather, nurture, protect, and restore the city how He wants.

In Matthew 23:39, Jesus made another staggering statement:

---

[1] See Psalm 2:8.

*For I tell you, you will not see me again, until you say, "Blessed is he who comes in the name of the Lord."*

When Jesus told the religious leaders of Jerusalem they would not see Him again, He was referring to something very specific. Jesus was not saying they would not see Him in any way because He was going to be publicly crucified in a few days. This statement is a reference to Jesus' triumphal entry into the city in Matthew 21. Jesus entered the city of Jerusalem the way Zechariah prophesied the Messianic King would[2] but was then rejected by the leaders in Jerusalem. Jesus was saying Jerusalem would not see Him enter the city again as King until He is welcomed and received as God's King.

Jesus refused to be King over the Jewish people until they willingly love and welcome Him, and He predicted a day would come when the leadership of Israel will welcome Him as their King. This means a day is coming when Israel will be saved, will love Jesus completely, and will invite Him to rule over her. *Jesus made His Second Coming and His rule as King from Jerusalem dependent on the salvation of Israel.* Therefore, a robust understanding of the Great Commission must include the fact that Jesus will not return until Israel is saved.

## Matthew 24

Matthew 24–25 gives Jesus' response to the disciples who were confused by the events of Matthew 21–23.[3] Because the disciples were Jewish, their primary concern was how Jesus would bring about the salvation and restoration of Israel. Jesus knew their deep desire for Israel's salvation, and He gave a startling prophecy which reveals quite a bit about how He viewed the Great Commission:

*And this gospel of the kingdom will be proclaimed throughout the whole world as a testimony to all nations, and then the end will come. (Matthew 24:14)*

The "end" Jesus refers to is the final sequence of events that ends with the salvation of Israel and the beginning of the Messianic reign. In Matthew 23:39, Jesus told the leaders of Jerusalem He would not

---

[2] See Zechariah 9:9.

[3] See Matthew 24:3.

rule until they welcomed Him. However, in Matthew 24:14 Jesus told the disciples He would not rule until all the nations received a witness of the gospel. *Jesus will not return and rule until Israel and the nations come to salvation. This is the strongest commitment He could have made to save Israel and a remnant in the nations.*

As Jesus continued, He affirmed His commitment to the salvation of Israel again:

> *Then will appear in heaven the sign of the Son of Man, and then all the tribes of the earth will mourn, and they will see the Son of Man coming on the clouds of heaven with power and great glory. (Matthew 24:30)*

Because of the phrase *the tribes of the earth*, Matthew 24:30 is often assumed to refer to the mourning of the nations at Jesus' judgments. It is true the wicked in the nations will mourn at Jesus' coming, but that is not what this verse refers to. It is a quotation of Zechariah 12:

> *"And I will pour out on the house of David and the inhabitants of Jerusalem a spirit of grace and pleas for mercy, so that, when they look on me, on him whom they have pierced, they shall mourn for him, as one mourns for an only child, and weep bitterly over him, as one weeps over a firstborn. On that day the mourning in Jerusalem will be as great as the mourning for Hadad-rimmon in the plain of Megiddo. The land shall mourn, each family by itself: the family of the house of David by itself, and their wives by themselves; the family of the house of Nathan by itself, and their wives by themselves." (vv. 12:10–12)*

Zechariah described a dramatic moment in Israel's future. It is the day Israel will see Jesus again, but this time she will see Him as the One who was pierced by and for her. The mourning Jesus refers to is the mourning of repentance among the tribes of Israel.4 When Jesus described the results of His Second Coming in Matthew 24, Israel's repentance is the first event He described. This tells us how significant that moment is to Him. *His return will do what no other event in history has done—it will save Israel.*

---

4 The word *earth* in Matthew 24 is a word that can refer to earth in general or a specific land. Matthew 24:30 is not referring to a sorrow in the tribes of the earth in general. It is referring to a specific time of repentance among the tribes of the land—the tribes, or families, of Israel.

Jesus' answer to the disciples in Matthew 24–25 emphasizes the salvation of Israel and the salvation of the nations. Jesus weaves together both themes in His message because He sees both as critical components of what we call the Great Commission.

## Acts 1

Matthew 24 is not the only passage where Jesus connected the salvation of the nations to the salvation of Israel. In Acts 1, Luke recorded a conversation between Jesus and the disciples just before Jesus' ascension. Jesus had taught on the kingdom for forty days, and the disciples had one question for Him at the end of His teaching:

> *So when they had come together, they asked him, "Lord, will you at this time restore the kingdom to Israel?" He said to them, "It is not for you to know times or seasons that the Father has fixed by his own authority. But you will receive power when the Holy Spirit has come upon you, and you will be my witnesses in Jerusalem and in all Judea and Samaria, and to the end of the earth." (Acts 1:6–8)*

After forty days of teaching, the disciples asked one question: "Will You at this time restore the kingdom to Israel?" This question is very revealing. The question demonstrates Jesus gave the disciples the expectation He would bring about the hope of the Old Testament— the fulfillment of the promises given to Israel in the form of a kingdom. The fact that the disciples asked Jesus if He would "restore" the kingdom to Israel means that the salvation they were referring to is connected to Israel's story. They were not asking about a new Israel.

We must see Jesus did not dismiss their expectation of a glorious future for Israel, neither did He correct their understanding of His teaching. As young Jewish men, the question of Israel's future was burning on the hearts of the disciples, so if Jesus wanted to redefine their expectation of Israel's future, He would have done that during those forty days. Jesus never had a problem rebuking expectations or beliefs that were out of sync with God's plan. But Jesus did not rebuke their expectation. Instead, He left a Jewish audience with the continuing hope that He would save Israel and fulfill what the prophets had predicted concerning Israel's future.

Many theologians argue that Jesus' First Coming was the fulfillment of all of Israel's promises, and that the kingdom of God takes on a radically different direction after the First Coming—a direction that no longer includes a restored kingdom of Israel. However, Jesus affirmed Israel's future and left the disciples with an expectation of a future kingdom for Israel. *If Jesus had fulfilled Israel's story in His suffering, death, and resurrection, He would not have spoken of Israel's restoration in a future tense.*

Jesus did not rebuke the disciples' expectation of a restored Israel, He simply gave them two very important pieces of information:

He addressed their expectations regarding timing. The glorious kingdom would not come to Israel immediately. It would take time.

He instructed them to take the gospel to Jerusalem, Judea, Samaria, and the ends of the earth. He connected Israel's restoration with the mission to take the gospel to the Gentiles.

The disciples longed for the restoration of Israel, so Jesus gave them an instruction to the nations, again revealing how deeply connected Israel and the nations are. If the disciples wanted to see the salvation of Israel, they would have to go to the nations. Israel cannot be saved without the nations' receiving the gospel, and the nations' receiving the gospel will result in Israel's salvation. In Acts 1, Jesus does the same thing He did in Matthew 24. He connects the salvation of Israel with a witness that must be given to the Gentiles. Jesus is making a simple statement: *Israel's story still matters, but it will be fulfilled in the context of the Great Commission.*

## Acts 2

Jesus gave the disciples a commission to go to the nations but told them to wait for the outpouring of the Holy Spirit.[5] Acts 2 is a pivotal chapter in the New Testament because it sets the stage for everything that follows. The event of Acts 2 sparked an explosion that continues to this day.

Acts 1 sets the stage for Acts 2. In Acts 1, Jesus connected the restoration of Israel with the mission to carry the gospel to the Gentiles. He also gave the instruction to wait for the outpouring of the Spirit to carry the gospel to the Gentiles. *The book of Acts tells the story of the outpouring of the Spirit to enable the gospel mission among the Gentiles for the sake of Israel's restoration.*

---

[5] See Acts 1:8.

*When the day of Pentecost arrived, they were all together in one place. And suddenly there came from heaven a sound like a mighty rushing wind, and it filled the entire house where they were sitting. And divided tongues as of fire appeared to them and rested on each one of them. And they were all filled with the Holy Spirit and began to speak in other tongues as the Spirit gave them utterance. (Acts 2:1–4)*

Though many consider Acts 2 the "birth of the church" there is far more going on in the passage. The way God poured out the Spirit revealed His ongoing commitment to Israel and His plan to include the nations in Israel's story. The outpouring of the Holy Spirit was a promise that had been given to Israel:

*Until the Spirit is poured upon us from on high, and the wilderness becomes a fruitful field, and the fruitful field is deemed a forest. (Isaiah 32:15)*

*"For I will pour water on the thirsty land, and streams on the dry ground; I will pour my Spirit upon your offspring, and my blessing on your descendants." (44:3)*

*"And it shall come to pass afterward, that I will pour out my Spirit on all flesh; your sons and your daughters shall prophesy, your old men shall dream dreams, and your young men shall see visions. Even on the male and female servants in those days I will pour out my Spirit." (Joel 2:28–29)*

*"And I will give you a new heart, and a new spirit I will put within you. And I will remove the heart of stone from your flesh and give you a heart of flesh. And I will put my Spirit within you, and cause you to walk in my statutes and be careful to obey my rules." (Ezekiel 36:26–27)*

*"Then the nations will know that I am the Lord who sanctifies Israel, when my sanctuary is in their midst forevermore." (37:28)*

*"And I will not hide my face anymore from them, when I pour out my Spirit upon the house of Israel, declares the Lord God." (39:29)*

The outpouring of the Spirit was part of Israel's inheritance. Jesus' promise to the disciples to pour out the Spirit was a commitment to give Israel her inheritance.[6] It was also a statement of His exalted identity. When Jesus poured out the Spirit, He was doing something only God could do, and this gave the apostles confidence He was who He said He was even though He ascended without saving Israel or judging the nations. It was one of the reasons the apostles preached to the Jews with such conviction. If Jesus could pour out the Spirit, then He could also do everything else the prophets predicted.

When God began pouring out the Spirit on the Gentiles, it was so shocking because the promise of the Holy Spirit was Israel's inheritance:

> *While Peter was still saying these things, the Holy Spirit fell on all who heard the word. And the believers from among the circumcised who had come with Peter were amazed, because the gift of the Holy Spirit was poured out even on the Gentiles. For they were hearing them speaking in tongues and extolling God. Then Peter declared, "Can anyone withhold water for baptizing these people, who have received the Holy Spirit just as we have?" (Acts 10:44–47)*

The Spirit fell on this Gentile audience while Peter was speaking to make the point that the Gentiles were now participating in Israel's inheritance in the Spirit purely based on faith in Jesus. There was no need to take on Jewish identity to receive the gift of the Holy Spirit. The Spirit baptized the Gentiles as Gentiles before Peter or any of the others who came with him could give the Gentiles any sort of instructions.

The apostles all agreed, if God was willing to freely give the Gentiles the Spirit, that was enough to indicate God had accepted the Gentiles into His family as Gentiles. This shows how significant the gift of the Spirit was to the Jewish apostles.

> *And after there had been much debate, Peter stood up and said to them, "Brothers, you know that in the early days God made a choice among you, that by my mouth the Gentiles should hear the word of the gospel and believe. And God, who knows the heart, bore witness to them, by giving them the Holy Spirit just as he did to us, and he made no distinction*

---

[6] See John 7:39; 14:16, 26; 15:26; 16:7, 13.

*between us and them, having cleansed their hearts by faith." (Acts 15:7–9)*

Because the promise of the Holy Spirit was such an important promise for Israel, the way God poured out the Spirit gives us a prophetic picture of God's plan to save Israel and bring her into her promises. Both where and how God poured out the Spirit are important. The fact God poured out the Spirit in Jerusalem is a statement of His commitment to that city. Jerusalem is where our story begins and where it will end. *God baptized a remnant in Jerusalem as a picture of a future baptism of the Spirit that is coming to the entire nation when He delivers them.*[7] The end-time deliverance of Israel and the accompanying baptism of the Spirit occurs in Jerusalem, and Acts 2 is prophetic picture of this day.

Luke repeatedly records that the Spirit fell on every believer gathered.[8] This outpouring was not just for a single leader or prophet. Acts 2 is meant to serve as a prophetic picture of the promise in Jeremiah 31 that a day is coming when every individual in Israel will know God because of the indwelling Spirit:

> *"For this is the covenant that I will make with the house of Israel after those days, declares the Lord: I will put my law within them, and I will write it on their hearts. And I will be their God, and they shall be my people. And no longer shall each one teach his neighbor and each his brother, saying, 'Know the Lord,' for they shall all know me, from the least of them to the greatest, declares the Lord. For I will forgive their iniquity, and I will remember their sin no more." (Jeremiah 31:33–34)*

Before Acts 2, outpourings of the Spirit tended to be for an individual to equip him for leadership or a ministry task. However, that all changed on the day of Pentecost. God began the process of fulfilling His promise to pour out the Spirit on every individual within Israel by pouring out His Spirit on every individual who was a member of the body. Therefore, the apostle John used the language of Jeremiah 31:34 in 1 John 2:27 to connect the New Testament outpouring of the Spirit with the fulfillment of the Jeremiah 31 promise:

---

[7] See Joel 2:28–29; Zechariah 12:10–12.

[8] See Acts 2:1, 3, 4.

*But the anointing that you received from him abides in you, and you have no need that anyone should teach you. But as his anointing teaches you about everything, and is true, and is no lie—just as it has taught you, abide in him. (1 John 2:27)*

Pentecost was also referred to as the *Feast of Harvest* because it celebrated the gathering of the harvest in Israel. Just as Israel began harvesting grain and barley at the time of Pentecost, the day of Pentecost reprints the beginning of God's harvest in Israel and the nations.

According to tradition, Pentecost was the time God spoke to Israel in the wilderness and gave the law at Sinai. The outpouring of the Spirit was a new "Sinai"-type moment for Israel. It was marked by wind and fire just as the law-giving at Sinai was. When the law was given at Sinai, the people were not able to approach the fire, but at Pentecost the fire rested on each one of them. Again, it is a picture of the day all of Israel will be saved.

Acts 2 is also a prophetic picture of God's commitment to the Jewish people and the role of the Gentiles in Israel's salvation. It is significant the first result of the outpouring of the Spirit was to give a witness to the Jewish people:

*Now there were dwelling in Jerusalem Jews, devout men from every nation under heaven. And at this sound the multitude came together, and they were bewildered, because each one was hearing them speak in his own language. And they were amazed and astonished, saying, "Are not all these who are speaking Galileans? And how is it that we hear, each of us in his own native language?" (Acts 2:5–8)*

Israel was given a witness of the gospel first. This is the priority in the gospel Paul spoke about:

*For I am not ashamed of the gospel, for it is the power of God for salvation to everyone who believes, to the Jew first and also to the Greek. (Romans 1:16)*

In Acts 2, God emphasized the point that the gospel was to the Jew first. If the outpouring of the Spirit was intended to transition Israel's promises away from Israel to the nations, then the first result of the outpouring would have been preaching to the nations. Instead, Jews were the first believers baptized in the Spirit, and Jews were the first to hear the gospel before the outpouring of the Spirit went to the nations. *God intends we keep this same priority as a part of our missions strategies.*

Not only was this a statement of Jewish priority, it also revealed a key purpose for the outpouring of the Spirit. The outpouring of the Spirit is not only Israel's inheritance; it is also the means of Israel coming into her inheritance. One of the purposes of the outpouring of the Spirit is to enable the Gentile church to give a witness to unbelieving Israel. Luke tells us the first witness on the day of Pentecost was given to Jews from "every nation under heaven" who heard a witness in their "native languages."

There are several key themes present in this moment. The first theme is God's mercy in Israel's judgment. The exile was God's judgment on Israel, and the fact that Jews still dwell in the nations of the earth remains a visible reminder of God's judgment on Israel. Acts 2 demonstrates God's gracious desire to redeem Israel even when she suffers the effects of His judgments. The Jews who heard the early believers speaking in tongues (or "languages") described these Gentile languages as their native languages.[9] *The fact that Jews refer to Gentile languages as their native languages is a result of God's judgment, because Gentile languages should be foreign to the Jewish people.*

Acts 2 is a prophetic picture of the Jewish people hearing the gospel during exile and judgment. This is a profound picture of God's commitment to pursue the Jewish people. When Peter stood up and declared that the promise of the Spirit was for "all who are far off," it was a reference to the Jewish people living in the nations. Peter recognized God's promise to Israel was still alive even though Israel had been scattered in the nations. Peter understood the outpouring in Acts 2 was great news for the Jewish people.

> *And Peter said to them, "Repent and be baptized every one of you in the name of Jesus Christ for the forgiveness of your sins, and you will receive the gift of the Holy Spirit. For the promise is for you and for your children and for all who are far off, everyone whom the Lord our God calls to himself." (Acts 2:38–39)*

---

[9] See Acts 2:8.

Luke described the Jews hearing this witness as coming from "every nation under heaven," which is another statement of God's intention to pursue the Jewish people in every nation in the earth. Amid global exile, He has not forgotten them. He will speak tenderly to them in the nations.[10]

The second key theme is a Gentile witness that must be given to Israel. In Acts 2, the Jewish pilgrims in Jerusalem heard the gospel in Gentile languages because God has a divine plan to provoke the Jewish people through a witness given through Gentile believers. *Acts 2 is a prophetic picture of Gentiles filled with the Spirit speaking the gospel back to Israel.* The apostle Paul develops this idea when he connects the gospel's expansion among the Gentiles to Israel's story by predicting that the Gentiles will provoke (make Israel "jealous") to return to her God.

> *So I ask, did they stumble in order that they might fall? By no means! Rather, through their trespass salvation has come to the Gentiles, so as to make Israel jealous.... Now I am speaking to you Gentiles. Inasmuch then as I am an apostle to the Gentiles, I magnify my ministry in order somehow to make my fellow Jews jealous, and thus save some of them. (Romans 11:11, 13–14)*

The expansion of the gospel to the nations will produce a witness that will be given to the Jewish people. The outpouring of the Spirit set all of this into motion.

> *Lest you be wise in your own sight, I do not want you to be unaware of this mystery, brothers: a partial hardening has come upon Israel, until the fullness of the Gentiles has come in. And in this way all Israel will be saved, as it is written, "The Deliverer will come from Zion, he will banish ungodliness from Jacob." (Romans 11:25–26)*

The third key theme is God's plan to unite Israel and the nations into one people. In Ephesians, Paul described God's intention to form "One New Man" out of Jew and Gentile.[11] The gospel will break down the barriers of separation that have kept Jew and Gentile apart for

---

[10] See Hosea 2:14.

[11] See Ephesians 2:15.

generations. Acts 2 provides a picture of God's plan to resolve the crisis of the Tower of Babel. The nations Luke lists in Acts 2:8–11, therefore, are likely an updated list of the table of nations from Genesis 10.

At the Tower of Babel, God separated the people of the earth through languages. In Acts 2, through the outpouring of the Spirit, languages will now be used in a redemptive way to call people from the nations back to God. The people of the earth who are deeply divided are being brought back into a single people. The judgment of Babel has been redeemed. God has revealed His plan to resolve the crisis that began in Genesis 11. *Language and culture are no longer barriers. Through the outpouring of the Spirit, unity and restoration are now possible.*

When Peter stood up to explain the phenomena of Pentecost, he addressed "Men of Judea and those who dwell in Jerusalem"[12] and "men of Israel."[13] This set the tone for his sermon. Peter directed his message to Israel, and therefore, his sermon interpreted the events of Pentecost in light of Israel's promises and future. In his sermon, Peter quoted Joel's prophecy because he recognized the connection between Acts 2 and Joel's prophecy that God would pour out the Spirit on Israel[14]:

> *"And it shall come to pass afterward, that I will pour out my Spirit on all flesh; your sons and your daughters shall prophesy, your old men shall dream dreams, and your young men shall see visions. Even on the male and female servants in those days I will pour out my Spirit." (Joel 2:28–29)*

Joel 2 predicts far more than what happened in Acts 2, but Acts 2 is the beginning of the fulfillment of Joel's prophecy. It has set the stage for the fulfillment of Joel 2. It is a guarantee the greater outpouring Joel prophesied will come.

Ancient Israel had "early rains" and "late rains." The early rains began the growing season and set the stage for the late rains which brought in the big harvest. Peter understood the connection between

---

[12] See Acts 2:14.

[13] See Acts 2:22.

[14] See Acts 2:16–21.

Joel 2 and Acts according to Israel's harvest cycle. Acts 2 was an early rain—the beginning of the growing and harvesting season—that would set the stage for Joel 2—the great harvest. According to Joel, a key component of the great harvest is the salvation of Israel.

This is the basis for Peter's statement in Acts 2:21. While it is true the gospel is now freely available and everyone in the nations who calls on the name of the Lord will be saved, Peter had in mind the day when everyone in Israel called upon the Lord for salvation:

*"And it shall come to pass that everyone who calls upon the name of the Lord shall be saved." (Acts 2:21)*

Peter's statement in Acts 2:21 is a quotation of Joel 2:32:

*"And it shall come to pass that everyone who calls on the name of the Lord shall be saved. For in Mount Zion and in Jerusalem there shall be those who escape, as the Lord has said, and among the survivors shall be those whom the Lord calls."*

Joel 2:32 is a direct reference to the prophecy of Zechariah 12:10–12:

*"And I will pour out on the house of David and the inhabitants of Jerusalem a spirit of grace and pleas for mercy, so that, when they look on me, on him whom they have pierced, they shall mourn for him, as one mourns for an only child, and weep bitterly over him, as one weeps over a firstborn. On that day the mourning in Jerusalem will be as great as the mourning for Hadad-rimmon in the plain of Megiddo. The land shall mourn, each family by itself: the family of the house of David by itself, and their wives by themselves; the family of the house of Nathan by itself, and their wives by themselves."*

The date of Joel's prophecy is not known, so it is impossible to say whether Joel is referencing Zechariah's prophecy or whether Zechariah is expanding on Joel's prophecy. Either way, Peter's audience would have understood his reference to Joel 2:32 to also be a reference to the prophecy of Israel's salvation in Zechariah 12:10–12. Peter's point is the outpouring of the Spirit in Acts 2 will result in the day when all Israel calls on the name of the Lord.

Because the church expanded so rapidly among the Gentiles, most people think of the day of Pentecost as the day God shifted His redemptive plan away from Israel to the nations. On the contrary, the day of Pentecost was an expression of God's commitment to Israel. The events of Acts 2 did not shift God's plan from Israel to the nations. Instead, it invited the nations into Israel's story and gave a prophetic picture of the witness the nations will give to Israel. *Acts 2 is not the end of Israel's story; it is a significant step towards the fulfillment of Israel's promises.*

Acts 2 is simultaneously a fulfillment of God's promises and a prophecy in and of itself. It predicts the day of a great outpouring of the Spirit which will accompany Israel's salvation. The outpouring of the Spirit has led to the salvation of the Gentiles in a way the Old Testament prophets would have never anticipated. However, the outpouring of the Spirit must also do what it was divinely intended to do from the beginning—save Israel.

Because God's redemptive plan unfolds over centuries, Paul warned the Gentiles against arrogance,[15] which he defines as the idea God is finished with Israel because of the success of the gospel among the Gentiles. God's process seems slow to us, but we must remember the words of Habakkuk:

> *"For still the vision awaits its appointed time; it hastens to the end—it will not lie. If it seems slow, wait for it; it will surely come; it will not delay." (Habakkuk 2:3)*

Luke recorded the events of Acts 1–3 in a very intentional way. In Acts 1, he recorded Jesus' prediction of Israel's restoration connected to the preaching of the gospel in the nations. In Acts 2, Luke connected the outpouring of the Spirit to the Acts 1 mission. In Acts 3, Luke recorded Peter's prediction that the outpouring of the Spirit will result in Israel's restoration. The subsequent chapters in Acts will primarily tell the story of the explosive growth of the church among the Gentiles. In these first three chapters, Luke establishes an important foundation: the salvation of the nations will play a significant role in Israel's salvation.

---

[15] See Romans 11:18, 25.

## Acts 3

In Acts 3, Peter spoke about the future fulfillment of Israel's promises:

*"That times of refreshing may come from the presence of the Lord, and that he may send the Christ appointed for you, Jesus, whom heaven must receive until the time for restoring all the things about which God spoke by the mouth of his holy prophets long ago." (vv. 20–21)*

Peter, like Jesus, stated there would be a time in the future when God restored "all things" as the prophets promised. Peter's statement was an echo of Acts 1:6–7. It gives us insight into what Jesus taught the disciples during His forty days of teaching, and there are several things we should note here.

First, Peter expected a future fulfillment of the biblical promises. In context, Peter was referring primarily to Israel's promises. This means the promises of the prophets were not fulfilled in the First Coming. Second, Peter used the same language of "restoration" Jesus used in Acts 1. While Peter didn't explicitly mention "Israel" as Jesus did in Acts 1:6, from the context he is clearly referring to Israel's restoration.[16] Peter would not have used this language of restoration if Jesus had taught a "new" Israel was coming without any connection to historical Israel.

Third, the word Peter uses for restoration, ἀποκατάστασις *(apokatastasis)*, is very significant. This is the word used in the Septuagint[17] for the future return of the Jews in the nations to the land of Israel. Peter used this word because, after the Babylonian exile of 586 BC, most Jews never returned to Israel. There was a remnant in the land, but the exile had not yet ended. This is why Paul regularly encountered synagogues and Jewish populations in his early missionary journeys to the Gentile world.

To this day, only about half of Jews in the world live in the State of Israel. The exile has not yet ended because the Jewish people have

---

[16] See Isaiah 40:9–11; Jeremiah 32:42–44; Ezekiel 37:21–28; Hosea 11:9–11; 14:4–7; Amos 9:11–15.

[17] The Septuagint is an ancient translation of the Old Testament into Greek used at the time of Jesus and in the early church. Many of the quotations of the Old Testament in the New Testament quote the Septuagint.

not been restored *entirely* to their land. However, the prophets all predict a time when God will bring all the exiles—the entire Jewish people—back to Israel from the nations.[18] The restoration of Israel requires all the exiles to be regathered to Israel—something that has not happened to this day. When Peter used ἀποκατάστασις to refer to restoration, he was referring to the return of all Jewish exiles to the land.

Finally, Peter said Jesus would restore "all" the things the prophets spoke about. Jesus' First Coming was a fulfillment of many prophecies, but it was not the fulfillment of all the prophecies. Peter's reference to the Old Testament prophets is a reference to their predictions concerning Israel and her Messiah. Peter was fully aware that Jesus, as the Jewish Messiah, should have restored the kingdom of Israel and regathered all Jewish exiles. Peter knew this was the chief objection his Jewish audience had to the idea that Jesus was the Jewish Messiah, so he used restoration language to tell a Jewish audience Jesus would bring about Israel's restoration. The apostles frequently challenged Jewish expectations about the Messiah and His suffering, so the fact that Peter did not confront their expectation regarding Israel is very significant.

Peter did not redefine Israel or challenge Jewish expectation of a restored Israel to validate Jesus as the Messiah. Neither did he explain Jesus' failure to restore Israel in His First Coming as a change in God's intentions regarding Israel. He affirmed the kingdom of Israel must be restored and the exiles must return and the rest of Peter's sermon on Acts 3 has this emphasis.[19]

Peter explained Israel's restoration in the same way Jesus did in Acts 1. Jesus' First Coming did not fulfill every promise, but He will return again to fulfill all that the prophets spoke.

---

[18] See Psalm 14:7; 102:13, 19–20; Isaiah 11:11–12, 15–16; 27:12–13; 35:5–10; 41:9; 43:6–7; 49; 52:11–12; 60:4; 61:1–3; 66:20; Jeremiah 31:8–10; Ezekiel 39:25–28; Joel 2:32–3:1; Hosea 11:11; Micah 2:12–13; 4:6–7; 5:6; 7:12; Zechariah 10:6–11.

[19] Luke's language in Acts 3:21 is also similar to his language in Luke 1:70 because the two passages are connected. In Luke 1, Israel's salvation is also the main theme in the fulfillment of what the prophet's have spoken.

## Acts 10

Peter not only affirmed the future salvation of Israel, he also recognized God's divine plan to save the Gentiles. Peter is often thought of as an apostle to the Jews, but the Lord gave Peter a profound experience related to God's intention to save the Gentiles.[20] As a result of the vision, Peter agreed to visit the house of Cornelius, a Gentile who was seeking the God of Israel. While at Cornelius's house, the Holy Spirit was poured out on the Gentiles:

> And he said to them, "You yourselves know how unlawful it is for a Jew to associate with or to visit anyone of another nation, but God has shown me that I should not call any person common or unclean. So when I was sent for, I came without objection. I ask then why you sent for me." ...So Peter opened his mouth and said: "Truly I understand that God shows no partiality, but in every nation anyone who fears him and does what is right is acceptable to him." ...While Peter was still saying these things, the Holy Spirit fell on all who heard the word. And the believers from among the circumcised who had come with Peter were amazed, because the gift of the Holy Spirit was poured out even on the Gentiles. For they were hearing them speaking in tongues and extolling God. Then Peter declared, "Can anyone withhold water for baptizing these people, who have received the Holy Spirit just as we have?" (Acts 10:28–29, 34–35, 44–47)

After the events of Acts 10, the gospel was no longer a message primarily for a Jewish community. It was a message for all people, and it began to rapidly spread among the Gentiles. Because of his experience, Peter played a significant role in the apostles' decision about how to relate to the Gentiles who had received the gospel. In Acts 15, Peter stood up at the Jerusalem Council and reminded the apostles God had accepted the Gentiles as His own people:

> And after there had been much debate, Peter stood up and said to them, "Brothers, you know that in the early days God made a choice among you, that by my mouth the Gentiles should hear the word of the gospel and believe. And God, who knows the heart, bore witness to them, by giving them the Holy Spirit just as he did to us, and he made no distinction between us and them, having cleansed their hearts by faith." (vv. 7–9)

---

[20] See Acts 10:9–16.

Though Peter primarily ministered to the Jews, God also gave Peter His heart for the Gentiles. *As an apostle, Peter carried both parts of God's plan—the salvation of Israel and the salvation of the Gentiles.*

## Revelation

The book of Revelation, like the book of Acts, predicts the salvation of the nations in relationship to the salvation of Israel. John began the book of Revelation with the prediction of the salvation of Israel:

> *Behold, he is coming with the clouds, and every eye will see him, even those who pierced him, and all tribes of the earth will wail on account of him. Even so. Amen. (Revelation 1:7)*

Like Matthew 24:30, Revelation 1:7 is a quotation of the mourning and repentance prophesied in Zechariah 12. This is not a prediction of the sorrow of the nations at their judgment, though that is a biblical idea predicted in other passages. Instead, John predicted the glorious moment when Israel comes to repentance and embraces Jesus. This moment of Israel's salvation was the first thing Jesus emphasized when He described His Second Coming,[21] and it is the first event John predicted in the book of Revelation.

These things reveal how central the salvation of Israel was to John. John introduces and summarizes the dramatic events of the book of Revelation as the events that will bring about the fulfillment of Israel's promises. The events of this book will cause Israel to embrace her Messiah in mourning, repentance, and deep devotion. John's expectation does not make sense if Israel's story was finished in Jesus' First Coming.

This emphasis on Israel and her salvation continues throughout the book. Revelation 7 and Revelation 14 describe a saved remnant from the tribes of Israel.

> *And I heard the number of the sealed, 144,000, sealed from every tribe of the sons of Israel: 12,000 from the tribe of Judah were sealed, 12,000 from the tribe of Reuben, 12,000 from the tribe of Gad, 12,000 from the tribe of Asher, 12,000 from the tribe of Naphtali,*

---

[21] See Matthew 24:30.

*12,000 from the tribe of Manasseh, 12,000 from the tribe of Simeon, 12,000 from the tribe of Levi, 12,000 from the tribe of Issachar, 12,000 from the tribe of Zebulun, 12,000 from the tribe of Joseph, 12,000 from the tribe of Benjamin were sealed. (vv. 7:4–8)*

*Then I looked, and behold, on Mount Zion stood the Lamb, and with him 144,000 who had his name and his Father's name written on their foreheads…and they were singing a new song before the throne and before the four living creatures and before the elders. No one could learn that song except the 144,000 who had been redeemed from the earth. (vv. 14:1–3)*

Revelation 11 predicts a day when two individuals will be anointed with incredible power to preserve Jerusalem.

*"And I will grant authority to my two witnesses, and they will prophesy for 1,260 days, clothed in sackcloth." These are the two olive trees and the two lampstands that stand before the Lord of the earth. And if anyone would harm them, fire pours from their mouth and consumes their foes. If anyone would harm them, this is how he is doomed to be killed. They have the power to shut the sky, that no rain may fall during the days of their prophesying, and they have power over the waters to turn them into blood and to strike the earth with every kind of plague, as often as they desire. (vv. 3–6)*

Revelation 12 describes a cosmic war over Israel and God's supernatural preservation of Israel.

*And a great sign appeared in heaven: a woman clothed with the sun, with the moon under her feet, and on her head a crown of twelve stars…. She gave birth to a male child, one who is to rule all the nations with a rod of iron, but her child was caught up to God and to his throne, and the woman fled into the wilderness, where she has a place prepared by God, in which she is to be nourished for 1,260 days…. And when the dragon saw that he had been thrown down to the earth, he pursued the woman who had given birth to the male child. But the woman was given the two wings of the great eagle so that she might fly from the serpent into the wilderness, to the place where she is to be nourished for a time, and times, and half a time. The serpent poured water like a river out of his mouth after the woman, to sweep her away with a flood. But the earth came to*

*the help of the woman, and the earth opened its mouth and swallowed the*
*river that the dragon had poured from his mouth. (vv. 1, 5–6, 13–16)*

*Though many aspects of Revelation 7, 11, 12, and 14 are up to*
*interpretation, these chapters clearly point to a future salvation of the Jewish people*
*and the ongoing significance of Israel in the redemptive plan.*

The book of Revelation ends with the description of the New
Jerusalem coming down from heaven to the earth. This celestial city
has the names of the twelve tribes of Israel on the gates and the names
of the Jewish apostles on the foundation. It is significant that all the
names on the gates and foundation stones of the New Jerusalem are
Jewish. If God intended to replace Israel's role in the story, we should
expect to find names from the nations there. Instead, the book of
Revelation ends with an emphasis on Israel's unique place in the
redemptive story.

*It had a great, high wall, with twelve gates, and at the gates twelve angels,*
*and on the gates the names of the twelve tribes of the sons of Israel were*
*inscribed—on the east three gates, on the north three gates, on the south*
*three gates, and on the west three gates. And the wall of the city had*
*twelve foundations, and on them were the twelve names of the twelve*
*apostles of the Lamb. (21:12–14)*

However, the book of Revelation also predicts the salvation of the
Gentiles. When John saw Jesus as the Lamb in Revelation 5:9, He
received worship because He is the One who has ransomed people
from every tribe, tongue, people, and nation:

*And they sang a new song, saying, "Worthy are you to take the scroll and*
*to open its seals, for you were slain, and by your blood you ransomed*
*people for God from every tribe and language and people and nation."*

In Revelation 7, the same chapter that describes the remnant saved
from every tribe in Israel, John saw a saved multitude from every tribe,
people, and language:

*After this I looked, and behold, a great multitude that no one could*
*number, from every nation, from all tribes and peoples and languages,*
*standing before the throne and before the Lamb, clothed in white robes,*
*with palm branches in their hands. (v. 9)*

The book of Revelation could be considered the most dramatic book in the Bible, and it is introduced with a prediction of Israel's salvation and contains predictions of the salvation of the Gentiles. In the book of Revelation, both are the result of the Great Commission.

## One New Man

Many people believe God's purposes for Israel have ended because of the emphasis in the New Testament on God's plan to form the church as a people from all nations. The apostle Paul referred to God's forming the church out of many as His creating *one new man*:

> *That he might create in himself one new man in place of the two, so making peace, and might reconcile us both to God in one body through the cross. (Ephesians 2:15–16)*

Paul described God's plan to bring together Jew and Gentile into one people as the very *mystery of Christ*:

> *When you read this, you can perceive my insight into the mystery of Christ. . . . This mystery is that the Gentiles are fellow heirs, members of the same body, and partakers of the promise in Christ Jesus through the gospel. (Ephesians 3:4, 6)*

If God's plan is to bring Jew and Gentile together in a single people, then it would make sense to question whether Israel still has a specific purpose among the nations. To answer the question, we must look to the mystery of Christ which is found in God Himself.

God is often referred to as *the Trinity*, a term used to describe the fact that God is one, He is unified, and yet within the Godhead there are three distinct Persons: Father, Son, and Holy Spirit. All three are God and live in complete unity. The Godhead cannot be separated, yet there are distinct roles for each Person.

The church is formed in a similar way. It is a single body unified for a single purpose and bound together in love. However, within the body, distinct assignments can exist for people groups. Paul addresses three different examples of this in the book of Ephesians.

The first group is Jew and Gentile within One New Man. We assume that unity requires uniformity because people usually seek unity by making everyone the same. However, the glory of the gospel is that

God forms a unified people from the nations and those people retain elements of their diversity in this age for redemptive purposes.

The second example Paul uses is the ministry gifts in the church. Paul specifically names apostles, prophets, pastors, teachers, and evangelists[22] while emphasizing that these ministry gifts are given by God to build up and equip *one* body bound by *one* Lord, *one* faith, and *one* baptism.[23] God gives distinct ministry gifts to the church. Some are pastors, and others are evangelists. We need pastors to function as pastors, or else the body lacks something. We need evangelists to function as evangelists, or else we are missing something. When these different ministry gifts function the entire body benefits.

A third example group Paul refers to in Ephesians is husband and wife. The husband and wife have distinct and complementary differences. Both are equally loved by God, have equal access to the grace of God, and possess equal standing before God. However, they also have distinctions in this age, and those distinctions benefit the family. When the husband and wife function in their distinctions, the family becomes something more than it could be with solely a husband or solely a wife.

In each of these examples, we can see Paul's understanding of how Jew and Gentile function. There is one people before God. All have equal access to God. There are no second-class citizens. And yet in this age, there are distinct redemptive purposes God gives in the body. Those purposes are for the sake of the body, and when people do not function in those distinctions, the body is lacking something. This is pattern in God's own person that He has duplicated in His people, and it reveals how God can both form a single people, yet within that people, Israel can retain a distinct assignment with distinct promises in this age.

## Israel and the Nations: Deeply Connected by the Great Commission

It is true the New Testament describes the spread of the gospel among the Gentiles and gives a clear directive to take the gospel to the nations. However, *the New Testament does not treat the Great Commission to*

---

[22] See Ephesians 4:11.

[23] See Ephesians 4:4-6, 25.

*the nations as something completely new and disconnected from God's promises to Israel.*

Jesus did not redirect the church to go to the nations because He was finished with Israel. He sent the church to the nations because He remains committed to Israel. The Great Commission in the New Testament is a continuation of the plan of redemption announced in the Old Testament. The mission comes into much clearer focus and accelerates as the church is commissioned to go to the nations, but the essence of the mission remains the same.

The Gentiles have received an unprecedented invitation into the people of God, but it did not come at the expense of Israel's calling. A careful reading of the New Testament shows that God remains committed to a future salvation and a future restoration of Israel. The mystery of God's plan is that this salvation is deeply connected to God's plan to save the Gentiles.

# PAUL AND THE GREAT COMMISSION

## Paul's Perspective of the Mission to the Gentiles

We have looked at how the Old Testament set the foundation for the Great Commission. We also saw how the New Testament presents Israel's salvation as a future event connected to God's work among the nations. Now, we turn to examine Paul's view of Israel and the Great Commission. Paul has shaped the theology of the Gentile church more than any other biblical author, so we must grasp Paul's perspective of Israel's future and, more specifically, the role Israel played in his missiology.

Romans 9–11 is perhaps the most significant passage in the New Testament regarding Paul's understanding of the Great Commission. In these chapters, Paul discussed the relationship between Israel's story and the Great Commission in the nations. He explained his missiology related to Israel and the role the mission to the Gentiles plays in Israel's story.

Paul built his construction of missiology on his knowledge of the Old Testament. He had searched the Scriptures to comprehend the end of God's redemptive plan, and he used the Scriptures to interpret his mission. In Romans 9–11, he expounded on his mission to the Gentiles by summarizing prophecies from the Old Testament and using them as the scriptural basis for the commission he received from heaven.

By studying how Paul applied Old Testament prophecies, we can learn how to apply our understanding of the end of the age to the mission of the church. We have a tendency to view Bible prophecy as disconnected from missions, but Paul deeply integrated the two. We need to recover Paul's approach to Bible prophecy. Biblical prophecies are intended to give shape and direction to world missions by describing the result of God's activity in the earth. God gave those prophecies so we could labor with an awareness of what we are laboring towards.

## Paul's Grief

Paul begins Romans 9 with sober words:

> *I am speaking the truth in Christ—I am not lying; my conscience bears me witness in the Holy Spirit—that I have great sorrow and unceasing anguish in my heart. For I could wish that I myself were accursed and cut off from Christ for the sake of my brothers, my kinsmen according to the flesh. They are Israelites, and to them belong the adoption, the glory, the covenants, the giving of the law, the worship, and the promises. (vv. 1–4)*

This is the only time Paul introduced a statement like this. He made three very unusual statements:

1. He is speaking the truth in Christ.

2. He is not lying.

3. His conscience bears him witness in the Holy Spirit.

Paul gave three different declarations of the truth of his statement. The fact that Paul introduced his burden with three statements of this nature reveals the seriousness of these verses. Paul wanted to make sure readers did not treat his statement in Romans 9 as hyperbole. He wanted to make sure his words were taken literally.

Paul's unusual introduction was necessary because he used very strong language in the beginning of Romans 9. Paul said he had "great sorrow" and "unceasing anguish" in his heart over the issue of Israel. The word used here for anguish is the Greek word ὀδύνη. It can be defined as follows:

> ὀδύνη, ης f: (a figurative extension of meaning of ὀδύνη 'physical pain,' not occurring in the NT) a state of severe emotional anxiety and distress—"great distress, intense anxiety." καὶ ἀδιάλειπτος ὀδύνη τῇ καρδίᾳ μου "great distress in my heart is endless" Rom 9:2.[1]

---

[1] Johannes P. Louw and Eugene Albert Nida, vol. 1, *Greek-English Lexicon of the New Testament: Based on Semantic Domains*, electronic ed. of the 2nd edition. (New York: United Bible Societies, 1996), 313.

*odýnē means a. "physical pain" and b. "mental distress." odynáō is "to cause pain or sorrow," passive "to feel pain," "to suffer." The main LXX use is for deep grief of soul, as in Zech. 12:10; Is. 38:15; Am. 8:10; Prov. 17:25; Ezek. 21:11. In the NT Paul uses odýnē in Rom. 9:2 for his distress that his compatriots are shut off from salvation. In 1 Tim. 6:10 the reference is to pangs of conscience that afflict those who defect through love of money. odynáomai occurs four times in Luke and Acts. In Lk. 4:28 it is anxiety for a beloved child, in Lk. 16:24 torment at eternal loss, in 16:25 the anguish of remorse, and in Acts 20:38 the sorrow of final parting from the apostle.[2]*

We often try to grasp what Paul thought about Israel, but we cannot fully understand it unless we examine what he felt about Israel. Paul's burden for Israel was not sentimental. He was not burdened, confused, or bothered about Israel. He was in anguish. His pain over Israel caused him deep mental, emotional, and physical pain.

Not only was Paul in anguish, he was in "unceasing" anguish. He could not escape the pain he felt over Israel. He carried a burden for the Gentile churches and wept over them, but this was something different. His pain over Israel was constantly pressing his mind and emotions. The language Paul used describes what happens when a person experiences deep loss or a great tragedy, and because of grief, it is impossible to live life normally. Paul's grief over Israel was so severe he wished he could be cut off from salvation if it would result in Israel's salvation.

*If God were finished with Israel, Paul would not be in this kind of anguish over her situation.* This pain explains in part why Paul always went to the synagogue when he first entered a city. Going to the synagogue was not merely a practical starting place in a city; Paul had a burning desire for Israel's salvation. Paul was bold enough to claim he did not receive his gospel from any man but by direct revelation from Jesus.[3] He also stated the Holy Spirit bore witness to his burden over Israel.[4]

---

[2] Gerhard Kittel, Gerhard Friedrich and Geoffrey William Bromiley, *Theological Dictionary of the New Testament* (Grand Rapids, MI: W.B. Eerdmans, 1985), 673.

[3] See Galatians 1:12.

[4] See Romans 9:1.

Therefore, Paul's anguish over Israel is not his anguish alone. It is also the Lord's burden over Israel.

What the Lord did with Paul was very unique. Paul always had a zeal for his people. This zeal is what motivated him to persecute Christians. Two unique things happened to Paul after his incredible encounter with Jesus on the road to Damascus. First, Paul's zeal was transformed into anguish. He recognized Israel's deep need of salvation. Paul had a zeal for Israel according to his own understanding, but the Lord gave Paul His own burden over Israel, and it transformed the way Paul saw his own people.

Second, God took the man with a zeal for his own people and gave him a command to go to another people. This assignment was very unusual because Paul would have been the perfect man to send to Israel. He had a zeal over Israel and an anguish from the Lord for her salvation. However, God wanted Paul to receive and express God's full heart. Paul needed to love Israel *and* the nations, so God sent Paul to a people he previously despised.

Before his conversion, Paul considered Gentiles to be enemies and oppressors—an unclean people who worshipped pagan gods. However, the Gentiles Paul despised before his conversion became some of his best friends. He wept for their families and poured out his life for their salvation. He wrote his letters to the Gentiles with deep emotion, and his love was expressed in deep and tangible ways in his deep suffering for the sake of the Gentiles.[5] *Paul, in his life and ministry, became a picture of God's passion for Israel and God's desire for the nations.*

Because he was called to be a model apostle for generations who would follow, the Lord had to give Paul His entire heart. Paul's anguish for Israel was not in conflict with his burden for the salvation of the Gentiles. Paul did not carry one or the other, and neither should we. *Like Paul, we need to carry both parts of God's heart—anguish over Israel with a burden for the nations.*

When the gospel mission began, God had to give men like Peter and Paul His burden for the Gentiles. *In our generation, we need the opposite: We need God to give us His burden for Israel.* Their perspective of God's mission was limited to Israel's future until God enlarged their vision and their hearts. Our perspective has become limited as well. Just as

---

[5] See Acts 9:16; 2 Corinthians 6:4–5; 11:23–28.

God gave Paul a burden for the nations, He also wants to give the nations anguish over Israel. Like Paul, we need both parts of God's heart to have a complete vision of the Great Commission. In Romans 9–11, Paul does more than describe his anguish over Israel. He explains how his mission to the Gentiles will play a part in Israel's salvation.

## Paul's Predicament

When Paul wrote Romans 9–11, Paul addressed an issue that he faced throughout his apostolic ministry. He was traveling among the Gentiles, preaching they must submit to Israel's Messianic King. However, this message faced two major challenges. First, the nations were not impressed with Israel which, at the time, was a small people group under Roman occupation. Second, Israel had not received Jesus as King, so why should Gentiles embrace Israel's King when Israel had not? It appeared Israel's Messiah had failed to bring Israel into her promises, so how could Gentiles be certain Jesus was a true Messiah?

To understand Romans 9 in context, we need to recognize Paul was writing to Gentiles and Jews to explain how Israel will embrace Messiah and be saved. Paul is explaining how the promise of Israel's salvation[6] will be fulfilled to give Jewish and Gentile believers courage that Jesus is in fact the promised Messiah.

Paul began by reminding his readers of Israel's unique role in the redemptive plan:

> *They are Israelites, and to them belong the adoption, the glory, the covenants, the giving of the law, the worship, and the promises. To them belong the patriarchs, and from their race, according to the flesh, is the Christ, who is God over all, blessed forever. Amen. (Romans 9:4–5)*

Paul's affirmation of Israel's promises in Romans 9:4 set the context for Paul's message: Israel was in crisis but God will bring her to the point where she receives her salvation. As God reaffirmed His promises to Israel in the wilderness after she broke covenant by

---

[6] See Deuteronomy 30:1–6; Isaiah 4:3; 45:17, 25; 54:13; 59:21; 60:21; Jeremiah 31:34; 32:40; Ezekiel 20:40; 39:22, 28–29; Joel 2:26; Zechariah 12:13.

worshipping the golden calf,[7] Paul reaffirmed God's promise to deliver Israel even after her rejection of Messiah:

*They are Israelites, and to them belong the adoption, the glory, the covenants, the giving of the law, the worship, and the promises. (Romans 9:4)*

*And in this way all Israel will be saved, as it is written, "The Deliverer will come from Zion, he will banish ungodliness from Jacob"; "and this will be my covenant with them when I take away their sins." (11:26–27)*

*As regards the gospel, they are enemies for your sake. But as regards election, they are beloved for the sake of their forefathers. For the gifts and the calling of God are irrevocable. For just as you were at one time disobedient to God but now have received mercy because of their disobedience, so they too have now been disobedient in order that by the mercy shown to you they also may now receive mercy. (vv. 28–31)*

In Romans 9:6–12 Paul used Israel's history to make his argument. He used Ishmael and Esau as examples of people who should have received blessing because they were born into the covenant family but lost that blessing. Paul used those historical examples to make two key points:

This is not the first time in Israel's history that those who were positioned to participate in the promises of God suffered loss due to their rejection of God's plan.

God divinely elects individuals for His specific purposes. When we reject His divine election, we can be cut off from His redemptive purposes. Ishmael and Esau were cut off because they rejected God's decision to choose their respective brothers for a unique redemptive role. (Stephen made this same point in his sermon in Acts by reminding his audience Israel's rebellion in the wilderness was connected to her rejection of Moses as God's chosen leader.[8])

Paul used these stories to illustrate a point about Israel's tragic situation. Ishmael and Esau were born in the family but rejected the one God chose to bring about the family calling. In the same way, Israel

---

[7] See Exodus 33:1

[8] See Acts 7:35–53

rejected Jesus as the one God chose to bring about Israel's calling. As a result, many who were born into Israel and, therefore, should receive great blessing were being cut off from that blessing. Paul expressed this by saying not all who are physical descendants of Israel belong to Israel.

> *But it is not as though the word of God has failed. For not all who are descended from Israel belong to Israel. (Romans 9:6)*

Paul's conclusion was simple. Israel's rejection of Jesus is painful and shocking but not unprecedented. When you look at Israel's history, many of her key figures were, at one time or another, rejected by their family including Isaac, Jacob, Moses, David, Jeremiah, etc. *Israel's situation was a tragedy—and Paul was in anguish over it—but it was not a failure of the Word of God.*

In Romans 9, Paul acknowledged Israel, as a nation born to receive the gospel[9] yet rejected Jesus, suffered a tremendous loss in the process. However, it is not the end of the story. God will bring redemption out of tragedy. He is weaving a story in which Israel's tragedy will bring blessing to the nations and set the stage for her salvation through the Great Commission.

## Paul's Missiology

In Romans 10, Paul explained his missiology and the role the mission to the Gentiles plays in fulfilling God's promises to Israel. Paul began Romans 10 by identifying Israel's primary need—salvation:

> *Brothers, my heart's desire and prayer to God for them is that they may be saved. For I bear them witness that they have a zeal for God, but not according to knowledge. (vv. 1–2)*

God has opened a window of mercy for all who call on Him, and that offer of mercy is what will ultimately bring His plan to pass:

> *For there is no distinction between Jew and Greek; for the same Lord is Lord of all, bestowing his riches on all who call on him. For "everyone who calls on the name of the Lord will be saved." (vv. 12–13)*

---

[9] See Romans 9:4–5.

As Paul continued his argument in Romans 10, he explained how God's offer of mercy to all would play a critical role in Israel's salvation. To make his point, Paul referred to several Old Testament passages. To understand Paul's use of these passages, we have to keep a few things in mind.

We must remember the original context of these passages. Paul added new meaning to these passages, but he did not reinterpret them. On the contrary, Paul used the original context of these passages to make his argument. We also should remember Paul was a Jewish teacher. Referring to part of a passage and expecting the audience to know the entire context was a common teaching style in Paul's day. Paul frequently taught along these lines, and he expected his reader to understand the original context of passages he quoted and use that understanding to interpret his use of passages.

Paul brought light to Old Testament passages, but he did not completely reinterpret them. Paul frequently revealed that Old Testament passages meant more than the prophets understood them to mean, but he did not empty those passages of their original meaning. In Paul's time, the Old Testament was the only Bible the church had, and Christians were very familiar with it. In our time, most Christians are unfamiliar with the Old Testament, and we can easily miss the full meaning of Paul's teaching. Paul's use of the Old Testament gives us insight into his thinking. When Paul quoted an Old Testament passage, it reveals what he thought about a subject.

In Romans 10:11–13, Paul began to introduce the way Israel's crisis would be resolved through an interesting use of Old Testament prophecies:

> For the Scripture says, "Everyone who believes in him will not be put to shame." For there is no distinction between Jew and Greek; for the same Lord is Lord of all, bestowing his riches on all who call on him. For "everyone who calls on the name of the Lord will be saved."

Verse 11 is a reference to a statement Paul made earlier in Romans 9:33:

> As it is written, "Behold, I am laying in Zion a stone of stumbling, and a rock of offense; and whoever believes in him will not be put to shame."

Romans 9:33 is an interesting verse because it is a combination of Isaiah's prophecies in Isaiah 8:14 and Isaiah 28:16:

*And he will become a sanctuary and a stone of offense and a rock of stumbling to both houses of Israel, a trap and a snare to the inhabitants of Jerusalem. (8:14)*

*Therefore thus says the Lord God, "Behold, I am the one who has laid as a foundation in Zion, a stone, a tested stone, a precious cornerstone, of a sure foundation: 'Whoever believes will not be in haste.'" (28:16)*

Paul put these two prophecies together to make an important point in Romans 9:33 and 10:11. God has become a cornerstone of deliverance for Israel in the person of Jesus. However, that cornerstone is controversial and has caused stumbling and offense to many in Israel. Paul's point was Jesus is God's offer of salvation, but the offer of salvation is so controversial many in Israel will reject it—just as Isaiah predicted.

In verse 12, Paul stated the offer of salvation the prophets predicted is available to all who call on the Lord—both Jews and Gentiles. God's offer of salvation still has a unique promise for Israel, but He has also extended an offer of salvation to the nations. This is part of Paul's grasp of the mystery of the gospel.[10] It set the stage for verse 13.

In verse 13, Paul quoted Joel 2:32:

*And it shall come to pass that everyone who calls on the name of the Lord shall be saved. For in Mount Zion and in Jerusalem there shall be those who escape, as the Lord has said, and among the survivors shall be those whom the Lord calls.*

Joel 2:32 is part of a prophecy Joel gave that describes the day God delivers Israel, judges the nations, and pours out His Spirit on all of Israel. Contextually, this refers to Israel's calling on the name of the Lord. The passage described Israel's great hope, and Paul referenced it to make a point related to her salvation.

Paul put a lot into these three verses, and his thought process becomes apparent when we look at the progression in them:

---

[10] See Ephesians 3:4–7.

Verse 11—God is going to freely offer salvation, but the one He chooses will be a "stone of stumbling" and a "rock of offense." This is a prophetic statement of Israel's response to Jesus.

Verse 12—God is going to freely offer salvation to Israel and the nations. Amid Israel's rejection of Jesus, salvation will also be extended to the nations.

Verse 13—This offer of salvation to both Jew and Gentile is going to set the stage for the fulfillment of Joel's prophecy of a day when all of Israel calls on the name of the Lord for salvation.

Paul did not redefine the specific application of Joel 2:32 to Israel; instead, he explained that Joel's prophecy depends on the offer of salvation being given to both Jew and Gentile. Romans 10:11–13 is Paul's summary of his mission, and he then expounded on it in the verses that followed.

In Romans 10:14–15, Paul quoted Isaiah 52:7:

*How beautiful upon the mountains are the feet of him who brings good news, who publishes peace, who brings good news of happiness, who publishes salvation, who says to Zion, "Your God reigns." (Isaiah 52:7)*

*How then will they call on him in whom they have not believed? And how are they to believe in him of whom they have never heard? And how are they to hear without someone preaching? And how are they to preach unless they are sent? As it is written, "How beautiful are the feet of those who preach the good news!" (Romans 10:14–15)*

Isaiah 52:7 in context is a prophecy concerning preaching to Israel in the nations about the greatness of her God. Paul wanted us to apply Romans 10:14–15 to the nations because he has already said, in verse 12, Israel's message of salvation must be preached to both Jew and Gentile. However, that is a secondary application of Isaiah's prophecy. In context, Isaiah prophesied about Israel, and we must recognize Paul is using the verse in the same context.

Paul's primary application of Isaiah's prophecy is not preaching to the Gentiles. It is preaching to Israel. When Paul referred to "they" in Romans 10:14–15, he was referring to Israel. We know this for three key reasons:

1. It is the context of Isaiah's prophecy, and Paul does not redefine that context (though he expanded the preaching of salvation to the nations as well as Israel in Romans 10:12).

2. Romans 10:14–15 is an introduction to Romans 10:16–21, and the two must be interpreted together. As Paul's argument built in Romans 10:16–21, it became clear the "they" he was talking about was Israel.

3. Paul ended Romans 10 and began Romans 11 by describing God's plan to use the Gentiles to speak the gospel back to Israel.

This does not mean there is not an application of the passage for preaching the gospel to the Gentiles. Paul himself was driven by the ambition to preach the gospel to Gentiles who had not yet heard it:

*And thus I make it my ambition to preach the gospel, not where Christ has already been named, lest I build on someone else's foundation, but as it is written, "Those who have never been told of him will see, and those who have never heard will understand." (Romans 15:20–21)*

However, when Paul described his ambition to preach to the Gentiles, he quoted Isaiah 52:15. It refers to the nations and kings of the earth as they hear news about the Messiah they had never heard. This is different from what Paul did in Romans 10. In Romans 10, Paul used a passage from Isaiah focused on preaching to Israel to make his case that the Gentiles are to speak the gospel to the Jews scattered in the nations so Israel will hear the good news of her salvation.

Romans 10:14–15 is about Israel, but it does imply Gentile salvation because, without preaching the message of salvation to the Gentiles, there will not be Gentiles who can give a witness to Israel in the nations. This is why Paul used a passage about Israel in Romans 10:12 and included preaching to the Gentiles. The mission to the Gentiles is implied in these passages. *Therefore, using these verses as motivation to preach to the Gentiles is a valid application, but we must recognize these verses ultimately describe Israel's salvation.*

Isaiah 52:7 originally referred to messengers bringing Jewish exiles good news about their redemption. It was a message of salvation carried to the Jews in the nations. That context is why Paul used the passage in Romans 10:15 to make his point. *Because Israel was scattered among the Gentiles, she needed to hear the good news of her salvation from messengers in the nations.* Paul understood Gentiles were called to be messengers in the nations, speaking a message of salvation to the Jewish people. Therefore, the evangelization of the nations in obedience to the Great Commission will become a key component of Israel's salvation.

Paul anticipated Gentiles would question if this witness was necessary because Israel was the first one to hear the news of salvation. Israel also had a covenant history with God. Did Israel really need another witness? Here's Paul's response:

> *But they have not all obeyed the gospel. For Isaiah says, "Lord, who has believed what he has heard from us?" So faith comes from hearing, and hearing through the word of Christ. But I ask, have they not heard? Indeed they have, for "Their voice has gone out to all the earth, and their words to the ends of the world." (Romans 10:16–18)*

Paul's answer to this argument was clear: Israel has heard but must hear again because God wants to show mercy to her.

*One of Israel's primary punishments for disobedience was exile from the land, and Israel's presence among the nations is a sign of her judgment.* Even today the fact that nearly half of the Jewish people live in the nations is a statement about Israel's relationship with God. According to Paul, speaking to Israel about her salvation and her God is the biblical response to Israel's judgment in the nations. Tragically, the church has more often either ignored or persecuted Israel when we are called to extend God's mercy to Israel by speaking to her about her salvation.

Paul took the mission he introduced in verses 14–15 and developed it in greater detail in verses 19–21 by demonstrating how the Old Testament predicted a day would come when Gentiles would provoke Israel. He began by quoting Deuteronomy in Romans 10:19:

> *But I ask, did Israel not understand? First Moses says, "I will make you jealous of those who are not a nation; with a foolish nation I will make you angry."*

Here is the scripture he referenced from Deuteronomy:

> *And he said, "I will hide my face from them; I will see what their end will be, for they are a perverse generation, children in whom is no faithfulness.*

*They have made me jealous with what is no god; they have provoked me to anger with their idols. So I will make them jealous with those who are no people; I will provoke them to anger with a foolish nation." (32:20–21)*

In Deuteronomy, Moses prophesied Israel would provoke God to jealousy and anger by going after other gods. God often spoke of His relationship to Israel as a marriage[11]; therefore, Israel's unfaithfulness will drive God to jealousy. His response to Israel's idolatry is poetic and unusual. Israel made God jealous by going after false gods, so God is going to make Israel jealous by going after another people. Israel worshipped gods who are "no god." As a result, God is going to pursue a people who are "no people" to provoke her.

Paul interpreted Moses' prophecy as a prediction of the gospel going to the Gentiles. Israel provoked God to anger by rejecting His salvation. God responded by revealing Himself to the Gentiles—the ones who were not part of a covenant people. However, God's pursuit of the Gentiles was not a rejection of Israel. God did not break covenant with Israel; on the contrary, He simply expanded His covenant to include the Gentiles. Moses' prophecy is profound: God will use Israel's idolatry to save the nations and then use the nations to provoke Israel to return to Him. This is key to understanding the Great Commission. *God is pursuing the nations because He loves the nations and because He wants to show mercy to Israel.*

When Israel sees Gentiles experiencing the benefits of her inheritance, it is meant to provoke her. It is the classic situation of the child who does not care about an old toy until she sees someone else playing with her toy. Seeing someone else enjoying something that belonged to her first immediately provokes jealousy.

In verse 18, Paul summarized Israel's condition by asking the rhetorical question, "Have they not heard?" However, Israel is going to hear again, and one of the ways she will hear is through Gentile messengers who participate in Israel's inheritance and speak to Israel about her God.

Paul continued in verse 20 by quoting Isaiah. Like Moses, Isaiah prophesied God would reach out to the Gentiles and use them as a witness to Israel:

---

[11] See Isaiah 54:5; Jeremiah 2:1; 3:14; 31:32; Hosea 2:7.

*Then Isaiah is so bold as to say, "I have been found by those who did not seek me; I have shown myself to those who did not ask for me." But of Israel he says, "All day long I have held out my hands to a disobedient and contrary people." (Romans 10:20–21)*

*I was ready to be sought by those who did not ask for me; I was ready to be found by those who did not seek me. I said, "Here I am, here I am," to a nation that was not called by my name. I spread out my hands all the day to a rebellious people, who walk in a way that is not good, following their own devices. (Isaiah 65:1–2)*

Paul quoted Isaiah because of the context of Isaiah 65:1–2. Isaiah 65 is the answer to Isaiah's passionate intercession in Isaiah 64, and that intercession was a response to Isaiah 63. In Isaiah 63, Isaiah was given a prophecy of Jesus as the great Deliverer of Israel who would destroy all of Israel's enemies:

*Who is this who comes from Edom, in crimsoned garments from Bozrah, he who is splendid in his apparel, marching in the greatness of his strength? "It is I, speaking in righteousness, mighty to save." (v. 1)*

Isaiah 63 describes God's judgment of the nations and His mercy towards Israel. It describes Jesus as the great Deliverer of Israel—the greater Moses—who will deliver Israel from all her enemies.[12] The dramatic promise of deliverance in Isaiah 63 is followed by Isaiah's intercession and deep distress over Israel's condition in Isaiah 64:

*Oh that you would rend the heavens and come down, that the mountains might quake at your presence—as when fire kindles brushwood and the fire causes water to boil—to make your name known to your adversaries, and that the nations might tremble at your presence! When you did awesome things that we did not look for, you came down, the mountains quaked at your presence. From of old no one has heard or perceived by the ear, no eye has seen a God besides you, who acts for those who wait for him. (vv. 1–4)*

---

[12] See Isaiah 63:1–6.

Isaiah 64 began with an intercessory cry and ended with Isaiah's passionate petition for the Lord to have mercy on Israel and bring her back to Himself:

> *Be not so terribly angry, O Lord, and remember not iniquity forever. Behold, please look, we are all your people.... Will you restrain yourself at these things, O Lord? Will you keep silent, and afflict us so terribly? (vv. 9, 12)*

Isaiah poured out his heart in Isaiah 64 and ended his intercession with a final question about Israel's condition, "Will you keep silent, and afflict us so terribly?" Isaiah stood waiting for an answer to his intercession, and Isaiah 65 began with God's shocking answer:

> *I was ready to be sought by those who did not ask for me; I was ready to be found by those who did not seek me. I said, "Here I am, here I am," to a nation that was not called by my name. (v. 1)*

God answered Isaiah's intercession for Israel: He would reveal Himself to the Gentiles. This answer must have been incredibly confusing to Isaiah. He was in pain over Israel, but God's answer was a promise for the nations. God's answer continued in verse 2:

> *I spread out my hands all the day to a rebellious people, who walk in a way that is not good, following their own devices.*

Paul explained the "rebellious people" God referred to was Israel,[13] and God is going to spread out His hands to Israel in mercy through the Gentiles. Saved Gentiles will be God's expression of kindness to the Jewish people when they are a rebellious people who follow their own way rather than God's appointed means of salvation. *Isaiah's prophecy was ultimately a prediction of God's plan to save the Gentiles for the sake of Israel.*

Paul argued in Romans 10 from the prophecies of the Old Testament that God was going to use the Gentiles in a significant way to bring Israel to salvation. Though Israel's rejection of Jesus seemed to be a failure of the Word of God, the reality was the Word of God had not failed. On the contrary, though the prophets did not

---

[13] See Romans 10:21.

understand it, the Word of God predicted what would happen to Israel centuries before it happened. They predicted Israel would stumble at God's chosen Deliverer. They predicted God would reveal Himself to the Gentiles. They also predicted the Gentiles would play a decisive role in God's calling Israel back to Himself.

*But it is not as though the word of God has failed. (Romans 9:6)*

Though Israel's refusal of Jesus was a devastating event that drove Paul to anguish, it was not a failure of God's promises, and it was also not the end of Israel's story.

Romans 10 is Paul's explanation for his divine commission to go to the Gentiles. He had great anguish to see Israel come into her promises, but he understood from the Scripture Israel would come into her promises by being provoked by the Gentiles. *In Paul's generation, there was not a Gentile remnant in the nations who loved Jesus and could provoke Israel to jealousy, so Paul understood the gospel had to spread among the Gentiles before Israel could be saved.* Paul placed priority on speaking to the Jewish people about Jesus, knowing a remnant would respond, but he also knew the salvation of Israel depended on the nations. Therefore, the most effective way for Paul to labor for the salvation of the nation of Israel was to work among the Gentiles until they could provoke Israel to jealousy.

As Paul worked among the Gentiles, his heart grew with deep love and affection for them, and his apostolic burden grew to encompass Israel and the nations. Paul began with a burden for his people and then received God's burden for the Gentiles. The Gentile church needs the same sort of revelation. *The church has a burden for the nations. Now, we need a burden for Israel.*

Because Paul knew the Scriptures, he knew Israel's salvation was part of the climax of this age and that it would play a part in the transition from this age to the Messianic age, when Jesus will rule over the nations from Jerusalem. He understood the return of Jesus and His rule over the nations were inseparably bound to the salvation of Israel.[14] Paul's anguish was also fueled by His deep desire to see Jesus return. We also need this deep longing for the return of Jesus.

---

[14] See Matthew 23:39; 24:30.

Paul's burden for Israel drove him into the Scriptures, under the anguish of God, to see what was required for Israel to be saved. *Paul looked at the predictions of the prophets to better understand how to cooperate with the plan of God, and we are called to do the same.* As Paul searched the Scriptures, he discovered the glory of the Great Commission and found what the Bible had to say about the task God gave him.

## Summarizing Paul's Mission

We can summarize Paul's understanding of his mission this way: *The free gift of salvation being offered to the Gentiles is neither the end of God's unique purposes for Israel nor the fulfillment of His promises to Israel but the unforeseen—and shocking—means by which God will bring Israel into her inheritance.* God loves Israel deeply and will do everything He promised in accordance with her divine election as a people, but He embedded a glorious mystery in the Old Testament: Israel's promises and salvation are inseparably bound to the Gentiles' obtaining salvation through Israel's promises.

God's plan for Israel's salvation is a "New Covenant" not like the covenant made with Sinai:

> *"Behold, the days are coming, declares the Lord, when I will make a new covenant with the house of Israel and the house of Judah, not like the covenant that I made with their fathers on the day when I took them by the hand to bring them out of the land of Egypt, my covenant that they broke, though I was their husband," declares the Lord. (Jeremiah 31:31–32)*

Sinai was a unique covenant made with Israel, and to participate in that covenant, the nations had to become a part of Israel which was what prominent Gentiles in the Old Testament did. Rahab and Ruth were examples of this. Because it is not like the covenant made at Sinai, part of the glory of the New Covenant is that it has become a means of salvation for the nations.

Paul had confidence to take the prophecies of Israel's salvation and invite the Gentiles to receive that same salvation because he understood the Gentiles would receive salvation through Israel's promises which is what God promised Abraham in Genesis 12:3. Not only can the Gentiles receive salvation through Israel's promises, the

Gentiles must receive salvation through Israel's promises to fulfill their God-ordained calling to provoke Israel to return to her God.

The nations now enjoy access to Israel's salvation; however, the nations must remember the New Covenant was given for Israel's salvation. The New Covenant is the means of salvation for Israel and the nations, but it has a specific purpose for Israel. That specific purposes remains.

> *"Behold, the days are coming, declares the Lord, when I will make a new covenant with the house of Israel and the house of Judah." (Jeremiah 31:31)*

God's plan will bring all the nations to humility. Gentiles will be called to submit to the God of Israel and recognize God's election of Israel. At the same time, Israel will hear the good news about her Messiah from Gentiles through the Great Commission.

## Paul's Warnings

After he explained the mission to the Gentiles in Romans 10, Paul gave several specific warnings in Romans 11 concerning arrogance, pride, and ignorance. He anticipated his summary of the mission to the Gentiles would be misunderstood by Gentiles who would interpret Israel's rejection of Jesus and their salvation as indicators Israel's story was over. Paul's warnings are sobering and especially important if we are on the threshold of being able to finish the mission to the Gentiles.

Paul emphasized God had not cast off His people. In fact, throughout Israel's history, there would be those like Paul who were part of a believing remnant. It would appear Israel was cast off for a season, but it would be only because the gospel must spread among the Gentiles to fulfill God's plan of bringing Israel to her salvation.

> *I ask, then, has God rejected his people? By no means! For I myself am an Israelite, a descendant of Abraham, a member of the tribe of Benjamin. God has not rejected his people whom he foreknew. (Romans 11:1–2a)*

*Israel has not been rejected; however, Israel must receive the gospel. This means Israel's situation is a missional issue and must remain a priority.* Paul expected the Gentiles to respond to Israel's situation by continuing to speak the gospel to the Jewish people.

Paul used the story of Elijah to make a crucial warning:

*Do you not know what the Scripture says of Elijah, how he appeals to God against Israel? "Lord, they have killed your prophets, they have demolished your altars, and I alone am left, and they seek my life." But what is God's reply to him? "I have kept for myself seven thousand men who have not bowed the knee to Baal." So too at the present time there is a remnant, chosen by grace. (Romans 11:2–5)*

Elijah came to a place of despair where he believed he was the only faithful one in Israel, and God counted this as intercession against Israel. Elijah did not perceive the righteous remnant in the nation, and this was a serious error. Paul warned us against making the same mistake by overlooking the saved remnant of Israel. Paul knew, if the Gentiles considered all of Israel to be apostate, this attitude would quickly produce arrogance and anti-Semitism.

God, in His kindness towards Israel, maintains a remnant by His own grace. This remnant is a witness to the Gentiles in every generation. God has not abandoned Israel's promises or Israel's future. The remnant is intended to keep the Gentiles humble regarding their place in God's plan. Israel's resistance to the gospel is not simply the "ignorance" of the Jews—it is a divinely orchestrated event. Therefore, we must understand how it came about, understand how it will end, and avoid any kind of arrogance towards the Jewish people:

*What then? Israel failed to obtain what it was seeking. The elect obtained it, but the rest were hardened, as it is written, "God gave them a spirit of stupor, eyes that would not see and ears that would not hear, down to this very day." (Romans 11:7–8)*

*So I ask, did they stumble in order that they might fall? By no means! Rather, through their trespass salvation has come to the Gentiles, so as to make Israel jealous. Now if their trespass means riches for the world, and if their failure means riches for the Gentiles, how much more will their full inclusion mean! (vv. 11–12)*

*But if some of the branches were broken off, and you, although a wild olive shoot, were grafted in among the others and now share in the nourishing root of the olive tree, do not be arrogant toward the branches.*

*If you are, remember it is not you who support the root, but the root that supports you. (vv. 17–18)*

In Romans 9, Paul told the tragic story of those who rejected God's election and ended up cut off from the family. In Romans 11, Paul warned the Gentiles not to reject the election of Israel either because of a lack of understanding or because of Israel's condition. Paul expected his Gentile readers to read Romans 11:17–18 in light of Romans 9 so that Gentiles would not be cut off from their participation in God's salvation due to ignorance, offense, or arrogance.

## Paul's Conclusion

Paul "magnified" or enlarged his ministry among the Gentiles and saw it as part of God's divine plan to provoke Israel to jealousy. Paul did not have to choose between God's plan for Israel and His plan for the nations. Laboring among the nations was not in conflict with God's purposes for Israel. It was a statement of agreement with God's purposes.

*Now I am speaking to you Gentiles. Inasmuch then as I am an apostle to the Gentiles, I magnify my ministry in order somehow to make my fellow Jews jealous, and thus save some of them. (Romans 11:13–14)*

We can summarize Paul's understanding of Israel by summarizing Romans 11: Israel is not cast away. All that the prophets prophesied about Israel will come to pass.

*I ask, then, has God rejected his people? By no means! For I myself am an Israelite, a descendant of Abraham, a member of the tribe of Benjamin. God has not rejected his people whom he foreknew. (vv. 1–2)*

The Gentiles must provoke Israel for Israel to come into her salvation.

*So I ask, did they stumble in order that they might fall? By no means! Rather through their trespass salvation has come to the Gentiles, so as to make Israel jealous…. in order somehow to make my fellow Jews jealous, and thus save some of them. (vv. 11, 14)*

Israel's salvation will usher in the dawn of the Messianic age and the restoration of creation.

*Now if their trespass means riches for the world, and if their failure means riches for the Gentiles, how much more will their full inclusion mean.... For if their rejection means the reconciliation of the world, what will their acceptance mean but life from the dead? (vv. 12, 15)*

The Gentile church cannot be ignorant of this mystery. If we are ignorant, we will not understand the ultimate goal of the Great Commission.

*Lest you be wise in your own sight, I do not want you to be unaware of this mystery, brothers... (v. 25a)*

God has a brilliant plan to bring together the salvation of the Jews and the Gentiles. The Great Commission is going to result in the "fullness of the Gentiles"[15] *and* the salvation of all Israel.

*Lest you be wise in your own sight, I do not want you to be unaware of this mystery, brothers: a partial hardening has come upon Israel, until the fullness of the Gentiles has come in. And in this way all Israel will be saved, as it is written, "The Deliverer will come from Zion, he will banish ungodliness from Jacob." (vv. 25–26)*

If we are ignorant, we will become wise in our own opinion, which, in context, means to have an inflated view of the Gentile church and an attitude of arrogance, ignorance, or animosity towards Israel. One expression of this is when we neglect Israel as a part of the Great Commission.

The pattern for Israel and the nations is also the pattern for the nations. No people group can come to its God-ordained destiny on its own. The salvation of each of our people groups will depend on the obedience of other people groups as they play their part in the global mission of God and vice versa. We are all deeply interconnected and interdependent.

When Paul finished his survey of the mission, he was stunned by the wisdom of God in intertwining the nations' salvation with Israel's salvation. Like Paul, as we better understand the Great Commission, it should cause our hearts to explode in worship:

---

[15] See Revelation 5:9; 7:9.

*Oh, the depth of the riches and wisdom and knowledge of God! How unsearchable are his judgments and how inscrutable his ways! "For who has known the mind of the Lord, or who has been his counselor?" "Or who has given a gift to him that he might be repaid?" (Romans 11:33–35)*

Paul was stunned at God's wisdom. If God can work such unexpected good out of Israel's fall, how much more good will He work when the time comes to fulfill all the promises He has made?

# ISAAC, ISHMAEL, AND THE GREAT COMMISSION

## The Middle East and the Great Commission

The Bible tells a story that begins in the Middle East. It predicts the redemptive story will also end in the Middle East. We live in the first generation in history where the events of the Middle East have a global impact, and this is the beginning of a shift in focus back to the Middle East. Because of the impact the Middle East has in our generation, it is important for us to understand all the Bible says about the future of the Middle East.

At this moment,[1] it is difficult not to despair when looking at the Middle East. The situation is dire and unprecedented and has now become the greatest refugee crisis since the end of World War II. The indigenous, historically Christian population in the region has been decimated through slaughter and forced migration. Though there are significant reasons for despair, there are also biblical reasons for great hope. One of those reasons for hope is God's plan to bring redemption out of the story of Isaac and Ishmael.

## Ishmael's Mistake

Like many stories in the Bible, Ishmael's story is complicated. In Genesis 16, Hagar was given the mixed prophecy about Ishmael's future:

> *The angel of the Lord also said to her, "I will surely multiply your offspring so that they cannot be numbered for multitude." And the angel of the Lord said to her, "Behold, you are pregnant and shall bear a son. You shall call his name Ishmael, because the Lord has listened to your*

---

[1] 2017

*affliction. He shall be a wild donkey of a man, his hand against everyone and everyone's hand against him, and he shall dwell over against all his kinsmen." (vv. 10–12)*

Ishmael was an answer to Hagar's prayers. God heard her intercession and gave her a son. However, her son's future would not be easy. Hagar was told Ishmael would face conflict and have a difficult future. Part of this conflict has been related to Ishmael's rejection of Isaac as the covenant son.[2] It is important to notice what the Bible does and does not say about Ishmael. The Bible is clear: Isaac was chosen by God as the miracle son of Abraham, but Ishmael was not rejected.

We must be very careful not to refer to Ishmael and his descendants as "Abraham's mistake." We should never tell a child he or she is a mistake, regardless of the circumstances of the birth. The same holds true for people groups. Even in circumstances that begin in sin, we look for hope, destiny, and purpose. The Lord spoke to Hagar twice about the future of her son to give her hope.[3]

Tragically, Ishmael and Hagar were forced out of Abraham's household. They were not sent away because God rejected Ishmael. They were kicked out because Ishmael was "laughing" at Isaac. Paul calls Ishmael's laughter *persecution* in Galatians 4, which tells us Ishmael was mocking his younger brother.

*But Sarah saw the son of Hagar the Egyptian, whom she had borne to Abraham, laughing. (Genesis 21:9)*

*But just as at that time he who was born according to the flesh persecuted him who was born according to the Spirit, so also it is now. (Galatians 4:29)*

Sarah saw Ishmael mocking Isaac and forced Abraham to send him and his mother away. They were sent away because of Sarah's jealousy to preserve Isaac's calling. Sarah was concerned Isaac's older brother Ishmael would try to threaten Isaac's destiny. *It was not God's rejection of*

2 See Genesis 21:9; Galatians 4:29.

3 See Genesis 16:10; 21:17–18.

*Ishmael that caused Ishmael to be sent away. It was Ishmael's rejection of Isaac that caused Hagar and Ishmael to be sent away.*

Ishmael's rejection of Isaac's election was very significant, but this is not something unique to Ishmael. Many nations have failed this same test and resisted or mocked God's purposes for Israel. Even in the church, many have resisted Israel's ongoing election. We must understand Ishmael's error, but also recognize how widespread the error is.

Ishmael's rejection of Isaac was a critical event that has had serious implications for Ishmael and his descendants. It is the part of Ishmael's story most people are familiar with, but it is not the full story. *We have to understand Ishmael's mistake and Ishmael's promise to understand Ishmael's future and God's plan to bring redemption despite Ishmael's sin.*

## Ishmael's Promise

The Bible frequently uses the names and lives of individuals as prophetic pictures of what will happen to their descendants. For example, Jacob struggles, wrestles with God, is delivered by his son, and eventually is transformed to "Israel." In his life, we see a prophetic picture of the story of the nation of Israel. A similar thing happens with Ishmael. Key events in Ishmael's life prefigure what will happen to his descendants.

Hagar had been a slave in Abraham's household. She was essentially property and had little or no rights. She did not even have a say in whether she had a child with Abraham. Giving birth to a son who would inherit his father's wealth and become great would have given Hagar a sense of meaning and purpose. It was her one chance at dignity. It's no wonder Hagar responded to Sarah the way she did when she became pregnant with Ishmael:

> *And he went in to Hagar, and she conceived. And when she saw that she had conceived, she looked with contempt on her mistress [Sarah]. (Genesis 16:4)*

Hagar's pregnancy suddenly gave her a sense of pride. She hoped this son would rescue her identity and sense of purpose. This caused her to look down on Sarah and strife filled Abraham's household. Sarah responded harshly to Hagar's pregnancy, and Hagar ran away until the Angel of the Lord sent her back to submit to Sarah. Hagar returned to

Abraham's household, no doubt hoping God would redeem her situation through her son.

Things did not go as Hagar had hoped. Ishmael's rejection of Isaac caused Hagar and Ishmael to be sent away, and this shattered Hagar's hopes. Because of her and Ishmael's sins, she was now an outcast who had lost her last chance at dignity and any kind of social redemption.

After Ishmael and Hagar were sent away, Hagar was filled with such despair over the future of her son she left him alone to die. This is an extreme reaction for a mother, and it reveals the depth of pain and grief Hagar experienced. She could not bear to watch her son die, which indicates she felt so hopeless she was convinced he would die.

> *When the water in the skin was gone, she put the child under one of the bushes. Then she went and sat down opposite him a good way off, about the distance of a bowshot, for she said, "Let me not look on the death of the child." And as she sat opposite him, she lifted up her voice and wept. (Genesis 21:15–16)*

As Hagar wept, the Angel of the Lord suddenly appeared to her with a powerful promise:

> *And God heard the voice of the boy, and the angel of God called to Hagar from heaven and said to her, "What troubles you, Hagar? Fear not, for God has heard the voice of the boy where he is. Up! Lift up the boy, and hold him fast with your hand, for I will make him into a great nation." (vv. 21:17–18)*

When Hagar had run away from Sarah in her despair, the Angel of the Lord appeared to her to give her hope.[4] This was the first appearance of the Angel of the Lord in the Bible which tells us how significant Hagar and Ishmael's story is. This time Hagar wasn't running away; she had been forced out. The fact that the Angel of the Lord appeared to her again to give her a promise and course indicates how serious Ishmael's destiny was before the Lord.

The Angel of the Lord promised Hagar that Ishmael would become a great nation. The word used here for greatness is the Hebrew word גָּדוֹל (*gadol*) is not a word that simply means numerous. For

---

[4] See Genesis 16:11–12.

example, the word is used to describe God as in "God is Great." It describes the nature of a thing. It has qualitative dimensions.

God's promise to Hagar was not only a promise of many descendants. He promised Ishmael's descendants would become a truly great nation. The purpose of this promise was to give Hagar courage that the boy's future was not entirely hopeless. It would not have been a comfort to Hagar to tell her Ishmael would have many descendants but that they would mostly be a wicked people.

In Genesis 16, Hagar was not given this kind of promise. She was given a prediction about her son's future that was a mixed prophecy of future conflict. However, in Genesis 21, God gave Hagar the promise her son's descendants would become great. Genesis 16 and 21 predict different aspects of Ishmael's future, and both are true.

Why did God give Hagar a different promise for Ishmael in Genesis 21 than he did in Genesis 16? It is very possible Hagar's response to the Lord in Genesis 16 set the stage for the promise she received in Genesis 21. In Genesis 16, Hagar's pride over her pregnancy had caused Sarah to despise her and treat her harshly. Hagar responded by running away from Sarah, but the Angel of the Lord stopped her in the wilderness. He spoke to her about Ishmael and gave her a difficult command:

> *And he said, "Hagar, servant of Sarai, where have you come from and where are you going?" She said, "I am fleeing from my mistress Sarai." The angel of the Lord said to her, "Return to your mistress and submit to her." (Genesis 16:8–9)*

The Angel of the Lord told Hagar to return and submit to Sarah. Running away from Sarah and then returning made her situation even more humiliating than it already was, but Hagar submitted to what the Lord asked of her. The Lord had chosen Sarah to carry the covenant child, and God asked Hagar to submit to Sarah because of Sarah's call, not on the basis of Sarah's behavior. *Hagar's submission to Sarah was an acknowledgment of Sarah's redemptive call.*

God's promise to Hagar about her son is likely the result of Hagar's willingness to submit to God's redemptive plan. The second time Hagar found herself in the desert, it was not her fault. She had been forced out of the household because of the actions of her son. In her humiliation, the Lord gave her a promise. More than likely one of the reasons the Lord gave her this promise was because she had submitted to His redemptive plan even when it was costly and difficult.

God's promise gave Hagar hope. Good would come out of her situation. Ishmael's descendants have become a numerous people, but they have not yet become a great people. The promise remains unfulfilled, but it must be fulfilled before the age ends. God remains just as committed to Hagar's promise as He is to the promises He made to Israel. As we will see, the two are directly connected.

Though Hagar was in tremendous agony over her situation, and had submitted to the Lord's command before, when the Lord spoke to her in Genesis 21 it was because of Ishmael's cry:

*And God heard the voice of the boy. (Genesis 21:17)*

Furthermore, Ishmael's name means "The Lord Hears," and his name points to his destiny. In light of the meaning of Ishmael's name, Genesis 21 is a prophetic picture of his destiny. He is called to intercession. Genesis 21 also gives a prophetic picture of how God will fulfill Ishmael's promise. Ishmael was in the wilderness because he had rejected God's purposes for Isaac. He was suffering because of his own sin. As he suffered, he released a cry, and the Lord heard it. Ishmael's cry is the key to his destiny. It is what caused the Lord to speak to Hagar.

It is not an accident that the descendants of Ishmael are known for prayer. The Lord is going to redeem Ishmael's calling. Much of the trouble the descendants of Ishmael have endured has been an attempt to destroy Ishmael's destiny. However, the Lord is going to bring the descendants of Ishmael to a place where their pain from feeling outside the family causes them to release a cry before the Lord. The Lord will hear that cry and fulfill His promise to make the descendants of Ishmael into a great people.

The second indicator of how God will restore Ishmael is found in the story of Hagar. Hagar was willing to submit to what the Lord asked of her, and this created the context for the Lord to speak a word of hope into Ishmael's story. Hagar's response in Genesis 16 resulted in Ishmael's promise. This is likely a picture of how God will restore Ishmael. He will bring the women to repentance first. He will draw women to Himself, and as they repent and come to salvation, they will play a critical role in Ishmael's salvation.[5]

It is important we understand this divine drama so as to grasp God's purposes for the nations as the focus of the church increasingly turns to the Middle East and the role the nations play in God's redemptive plan. God is going to release a breakthrough in the nations that will play a key role in the salvation of Ishmael, which in turn will play a significant role in the salvation of Israel.

## God's Plan for Family Redemption

Part of understanding the battle over Ishmael's promises is recognizing the grand story God has designed for family redemption. The family controversy that began in Abraham's tents is headed towards an incredible resolution, and this resolution depends on Ishmael's coming into his promises. The enemy knows the importance of this, and that's one reason why there is such a battle over Ishmael coming into his promises.

Ishmael's trouble began when he rejected God's election of Isaac as the son through whom Abraham's covenant would be fulfilled. As the older brother, Ishmael rejected his younger brother's calling. Consequently, he had to be pushed out of Abraham's household. This resulted in a deep sense of fatherlessness for the descendants of Ishmael. There is a deep wound from having been pushed out of the family, and it has caused tremendous suffering for the descendants of Ishmael. The enemy has attempted to destroy Ishmael and Isaac's destinies by exploiting this family crisis through envy, strife, and calamity. The situation looks hopeless, but the Lord is going to do something glorious, and Genesis 21 gives us a picture of what is coming.

In Genesis 21, Ishmael let out a cry—a cry for destiny—because he had been forced out of Abraham's household. As we grow closer to the end of the age, Ishmael's descendants, burdened by the pain of the centuries, are going to let out a cry, and the Lord is going to hear that cry and fulfill Ishmael's promise. The Angel of the Lord responded to

---

[5] As an example of how this might happen, women are often the first to embrace the gospel in oppressive nations.

Ishmael's cry in Genesis 21, and the Lord is going to respond to that cry again.

Through Jesus, a powerful remnant of Ishmael's descendants is going to be brought back into the family, and God's promise of greatness for Ishmael will be fulfilled. The saved descendants of Ishmael are going to be a powerful part of God's witness to Israel, and this is part of the poetry in God's redemptive plan for Israel and the nations.

Ishmael was sent away from Abraham's family because he rejected the one God chose. In the same way, Israel has been, in a sense, cut off from the family of God because of offense at the one God chose—Jesus. Ishmael's descendants were born to be part of the family of Abraham, and Isaac's descendants were born to be part of God's unique covenant with Isaac. Both are separated from their calling through offense at God's election.

However, in the days ahead, God is going to bring many of Ishmael's descendants back into the family. The son who was cut off from the family will be brought back into the family by embracing Jesus. God is going to use this to provide a powerful witness to Israel.

The people who were forced out of the family are going to speak tenderly to the descendants of Isaac who have also been cut off from the family. *The descendants of Ishmael are going to look at the descendants of Isaac and say, "God brought me back into the family through Jesus, and He can do the same for you."*

Paul described God's plan to use the Gentiles to provoke Israel in Romans 10–11, and Ishmael's story is part of this provocation. God will use the nations, but He is going to use Ishmael in a unique way to provoke his brother to salvation. We must understand this purpose to understand what God is doing in the Middle East through the Great Commission.

## Paul's Profound Prediction—Provocation

Ishmael's promise is part of the provocation of Israel by the Gentiles predicted by Paul:

> *So I ask, did they stumble in order that they might fall? By no means! Rather through their trespass salvation has come to the Gentiles, so as to make Israel jealous. (Romans 11:11)*

*Now I am speaking to you Gentiles. Inasmuch then as I am an apostle to the Gentiles, I magnify my ministry in order somehow to make my fellow Jews jealous, and thus save some of them. (vv. 13–14)*

The power of the gospel will flow through Gentiles who will express the love of Jesus back to the Jewish people, and the Jewish people will see something among the Gentiles only God can do. *Jesus will so transform these Gentiles that the Jews who encounter them will be able to find no other answer for the transformation than the God of Israel.* It will be a great demonstration of supernatural love that overcomes the natural and historical animosity between Jew and Gentile. It will be something that breaks down pride and resistance to the message of Jesus as Israel's Messiah.

Instead of fighting God's unique purposes for the Jewish people, the Gentiles will agree with God's promises and make it a priority to express God's love to the Jewish people as they contend for the Jewish people's covenant destiny. This will happen in such a way that it stuns the Jewish people. It will be so staggering that it will cause them to reconsider their resistance to Jesus as Messiah.

Paul predicted Israel as a nation will not be saved until the Gentile believers come into "fullness" and are capable of delivering this witness to the Jewish people.

*Lest you be wise in your own sight, I do not want you to be unaware of this mystery, brothers: a partial hardening has come upon Israel, until the fullness of the Gentiles has come in. And in this way all Israel will be saved, as it is written, "The Deliverer will come from Zion, he will banish ungodliness from Jacob." (Romans 11:25–26)*

God's plan is a mystery. The way He has chosen to bring salvation to the Gentiles and the Jews is a plan that no man would have chosen. It does not make sense to the human intellect, but "this is the way all Israel will be saved." *First, the Gentiles will come to fullness, second these Gentiles will provoke the Jewish people to jealousy to receive the same salvation the Gentiles have received, and finally God will save Israel.*

## The Implications of Paul's Prediction

While Romans 9–11 helps us better understand how Paul perceived the future of the Jewish people, these chapters also have profound implications for the future of the Gentiles. More specifically, Paul's prediction helps us to understand the future of the Great Commission in the Middle East.

Presently, almost 50 percent of the Jewish people live in the State of Israel. Based on the rise in global anti-Semitism, Jewish immigration to the State of Israel is expected to increase significantly over the next few decades. This means it is very possible we could see most of the Jewish people living in the State of Israel in the next twenty to thirty years.

The provocation Paul described in Romans 10–11 requires a depth of relationship and proximity. It requires more than the Jewish people hearing the gospel; it implies they encounter the transformational power of the gospel in the Gentiles they relate to and interact with. Therefore, if the majority of the Jewish people will be in Israel in the coming decades, it means that they will be provoked primarily by the Gentiles living among them in the State of Israel and in the Middle East.

Paul's prediction is not only a prediction of Israel's salvation, it is also a prediction that a substantial community of Gentile believers in the Middle East will come to "fullness"[6] in numbers and in the quality of their faith. The State of Israel is surrounded by the descendants of Ishmael, so Paul's prediction is a profound prediction of a great revival among the descendants of Ishmael that will result in a witness being given to Israel.

Paul's prediction is astounding when we consider the centuries of conflict between the Gentiles and the Jews, and more specifically between Isaac and Ishmael. In the coming days, we will see a great revival among the sons of Ishmael—a revival so great the descendants of Ishmael will speak to the Jewish people about their destiny. *A people who came into existence by rejecting Isaac's calling are going to end up speaking tenderly to Isaac about his calling and provoking Isaac to come back into the family through Jesus.*

Ishmael's salvation is extremely significant. Ishmael's salvation—becoming a great nation—will play a part in Israel's salvation which then plays a part of the return of Jesus. This explains the enemy's

---

[6] See Romans 11:25–26.

vested interest in preventing Isaac and Ishmael's salvation. However, God is going to bring them both to salvation for His purposes.

## The Promise of Redemption

The story of Hagar and Ishmael provides a profound picture of God's desire to redeem nations. Hagar was a woman caught up in a situation she did not choose. As a slave, she had no choice except to obey her master, and that obedience ultimately caused her to lose everything. Having a child was her one chance at redemption, but her pride and Ishmael's sin shattered any hope she had.

The Lord's promise to bring something good out of Hagar's situation is a profound demonstration of His kindness. Hagar did not see the fulfillment of this promise during her life, but the promise of greatness was a statement from the Lord. He would bring good out of a hopeless situation.

The Lord's response to Ishmael's cry is also a profound demonstration of the mercy of the Lord. Ishmael had two things against him. First, his birth was a result of a compromise by Abraham. He was not the miracle son Abraham had been promised. Second, he had sinned by rejecting God's choice of Isaac.

Hagar and Ishmael's story is a powerful story for all those who have been caught in a hopeless situation. It is a story that also gives hope to those who have rejected God's plan because of their circumstance. It gives us profound hope for wicked nations. God can redeem nations—even those who have sinned seriously and those who have had a seemingly wrongful start. It is fuel for the Great Commission. God is going to redeem every tribe and tongue. Every people group has a redemptive purpose in the plan of God.

There is a lot of work to do before we see the fulfillment of what Paul predicted in Romans 11, but the Bible gives us tremendous hope for the future.

# FINISHING THE GREAT COMMISSION

## Understanding the Great Commission

Because we live in the first generation in history where it is possible to evangelize every people group, it is critical we understand all that is required by the Great Commission. *The Great Commission is sometimes reduced to evangelism, but it is far more than evangelism.* It is a command to disciple the nations to obey everything Jesus taught:

> *"Go therefore and make disciples of all nations, baptizing them in the name of the Father and of the Son and of the Holy Spirit, teaching them to observe all that I have commanded you. And behold, I am with you always, to the end of the age." (Matthew 28:19–20)*

Until we have discipled nations to obey all of Jesus' teaching, we have not fulfilled the Great Commission. Matthew 24–25—known as the "Olivet Discourse"—is one of the key passages that helps us to understand what is required to complete the Great Commission because these two chapters are an answer to the disciples' question about what will be required for the return of Jesus.

> *As he sat on the Mount of Olives, the disciples came to him privately, saying, "Tell us, when will these things be, and what will be the sign of your coming and of the end of the age?" (Matthew 24:3)*

Jesus' answer took the mission to the nations and put it in context to everything required to end the age. This is an important aspect of the Great Commission that is often overlooked. *The ultimate purpose of the Great Commission is to prepare the earth for the return of Jesus.* Only evangelizing the nations, therefore, is not enough to fulfill the Great Commission. We must prepare them for what the Bible says will come. Passages like Matthew 24–25 give us key information about what is required for the age to end and Jesus to return, and we must disciple nations to understand and obey passages like this as part of the Great Commission.

Part of the task of the Great Commission is taking end-time passages in the Bible and discipling the church considering what the Bible says will come. For example, because the book of Revelation predicts the church will consist of people from every tribe and tongue,[1] we work to see the gospel reach every people group. *The closer we get to the return of the Lord, the more we must understand similar end-time themes so we can move the church towards God's finish line.*

## Matthew 24:14

Matthew 24:14 is probably the best-known verse in Jesus' sermon in Matthew 24–25:

> *And this gospel of the kingdom will be proclaimed throughout the whole world as a testimony to all nations, and then the end will come.*

Jesus predicted the "gospel of the kingdom" must be proclaimed throughout the world—to all nations. The "gospel of the kingdom" is a specific message of good news that must be proclaimed to all people. Understanding this verse in context helps us get a better picture of what it looks like to finish the Great Commission.

Matthew 24:14 is part of a narrative that begins in Matthew 21, when Jesus entered the city of Jerusalem, riding a donkey as the prophet Zechariah predicted the Messiah would[2]:

> *"Say to the daughter of Zion, 'Behold, your king is coming to you, humble, and mounted on a donkey, on a colt, the foal of a beast of burden.' "...And the crowds that went before him and that followed him were shouting, "Hosanna to the Son of David! Blessed is he who comes in the name of the Lord! Hosanna in the highest!" (Matthew 21:5, 9)*

The people were shouting praises to the "Son of David" as a statement of their Messianic expectation. Though the leadership of the city ended up rejecting Jesus, Matthew recorded this event as a prophetic picture of the day Jesus would be welcomed as the King of

---

[1] See Revelation 5:9; 7:9.

[2] See Zechariah 9:9.

Jerusalem. (Matthew's gospel was written to the Jews, so he referred to Jesus as David's heir multiple times.[3])

Matthew 21–23 contains the unusual events that followed Jesus' triumphal entry into the city. People had shouted praises as Jesus entered the city, but things quickly changed afterward. Jesus rebuked the leaders of Jerusalem and exposed their resistance to Him. Jesus entered Jerusalem as its King, but He was rejected. His response to this rejection was to predict He would rule in Jerusalem when He was welcomed.[4] Jesus affirmed His identity as the King of Jerusalem, but made His rule from Jerusalem dependent on the repentance of Israel. This background is required to understand Matthew 24–25 fully.

Matthew 24 begins with the painful questions of Jesus' disillusioned disciples. They had just seen Jesus enter Jerusalem in the way Zechariah prophesied the King would enter, but Jesus seemed to say it was not yet time for Him to rule from Jerusalem. Confused and shattered, they turned to Jesus to ask when He would establish His kingdom in Israel.

> *As he sat on the Mount of Olives, the disciples came to him privately, saying, "Tell us, when will these things be, and what will be the sign of your coming and of the end of the age?" (Matthew 24:3)*

Their question was simple: If Jesus' entry into Jerusalem was not the beginning of His rule on the earth, what would be required for His rule to begin? Matthew 24–25 is Jesus' answer to the disciples, and it is in context to their expectation of the promised kingdom of Israel. Jesus gave the disciples assurance the kingdom would come just as it was prophesied. However, there is also a task that must be completed before the promised kingdom comes. Matthew 24:14 summarizes the task, and it lays the foundation for the Great Commission.

## The Gospel of the Kingdom

There are many aspects of the kingdom that are all good news, but Jesus had one specific message in mind. The events of Matthew 21–23 set the context. The good news Jesus refers to in Matthew 24:14 is the good news Jesus will rule over the nations from Jerusalem:

---

[3] See Matthew 9:27; 12:23; 15:22; 20:30–31; 21:9, 15; 22:42.

[4] See Matthew 23:39.

*And this gospel of the kingdom will be proclaimed throughout the whole world as a testimony to all nations, and then the end will come.*

Every tribe and tongue must hear the good news that all the promises the prophets made regarding Israel's King will come to pass, and Jerusalem will be made a praise in all the earth.[5] The promise of a coming King who will rule from Jerusalem is central to the gospel—the "good news"—we are to carry to the nations.

The gospel is a message of hope, and the biblical gospel is more than the gospel of personal salvation. It is the hope of a coming King who will save Israel and the nations. *The promise of individual salvation is incredible, but the gospel is far more than that.* We must proclaim Jesus to the nations as a King just as the apostles did:

*"And Jason has received them, and they are all acting against the decrees of Caesar, saying that there is another king, Jesus." (Acts 17:7)*

Jesus' identity as a King is a central part of the gospel, and this is why the question of whether He was a legitimate King was one of the primary themes of the crucifixion[6]:

*Now Jesus stood before the governor, and the governor asked him, "Are you the King of the Jews?" Jesus said, "You have said so." (Matthew 27:11)*

*And twisting together a crown of thorns, they put it on his head and put a reed in his right hand. And kneeling before him, they mocked him, saying, "Hail, King of the Jews!" (v. 29)*

*And over his head they put the charge against him, which read, "This is Jesus, the King of the Jews." (v. 37)*

*And Pilate asked him, "Are you the King of the Jews?" And he answered him, "You have said so." (Luke 23:3)*

*Now it was the day of Preparation of the Passover. It was about the sixth hour. He said to the Jews, "Behold your King!" (John 19:14)*

---

5 See Isaiah 62:7.

6 See Matthew 27:11, 29, 37, 42; Mark 15:2, 9, 12, 18, 26, 32; Luke 23:2–3, 37–38; John 18:33, 37, 39; 19:3, 14–15, 19, 21.

Jesus' identity as King is so central in His death He died under a sign that said, "King of the Jews":

*Pilate also wrote an inscription and put it on the cross. It read, "Jesus of Nazareth, the King of the Jews." (John 19:19)*

*And over his head they put the charge against him, which read, "This is Jesus, the King of the Jews." (Matthew 27:37)*

*And the inscription of the charge against him read, "The King of the Jews." (Mark 15:26)*

*There was also an inscription over him, "This is the King of the Jews." (Luke 23:38)*

Every detail of Jesus' crucifixion was carefully prepared by God.[7] Jesus could have died under any statement, but as He suffered, His Father chose to describe Him as the King of Israel. This means His identity as the King of Israel is not a secondary issue; it is central to who Jesus is and should be central in the proclamation of the gospel.

*The good news of the gospel is more than personal redemption; it is also God's commitment to set His Son in place to rule over all the nations from Jerusalem as the King of Israel.*[8] Part of the task of the Great Commission is to proclaim the glory of God's King to the nations, and that message is going to produce a people in all the nations who love Jesus as a King and identify with Him and His kingdom more than they do the nationalities they were born with.

Before He comes in judgment, Jesus will offer every people group the chance to turn from their sin and embrace Him as King. This is an expression of the mercy of God. Because Jesus is returning as Israel's King, part of turning to Jesus is embracing Him as the King of Israel. When we fail to receive Jesus in this way, we are missing a key part of His identity.

## Must Be Preached

The good news of Jesus and His Kingdom must be *proclaimed*.

---

[7] See Acts 2:23.

[8] See Psalm 2:6–8; 110:1–2.

*"And this gospel of the kingdom will be proclaimed throughout the whole world as a testimony to all nations, and then the end will come." (Matthew 24:14)*

Jesus used the word *proclaim* because it had a very specific meaning. The word was used to refer to the activity of a herald in the ancient world. Heralds were necessary in the ancient world to proclaim the messages of kings.

Because there was no media in the ancient world, a king's message would be given to a herald who would speak it loudly for the people to hear. When a king wanted to come to a city, he would send his herald ahead of him to prepare for his arrival. The herald would carry the king's message and instruct the people to prepare for the arrival of the king.

Jesus described the task of the church in this way because the church is called to go into the nations of the earth and teach them to prepare for the return of Jesus. This is what it means to disciple the nations to obey all Jesus taught. *As ancient kings needed heralds to go before them, Jesus has ascended to heaven and given the church the task to go before Him and prepare the earth for His arrival.*

When Jesus came the first time, He was hidden from sight for nearly thirty years. When it came time for Jesus to be seen, God sent a man named John to prepare the people to meet Jesus. John pled with Israel to come into agreement with God so she would be prepared for the arrival of His Son.

Jesus is currently hidden from the sight of the nations, and the task of the church is very similar to the task of John the Baptist. We are called to prepare the nations for the return of Jesus. We plead with the nations to come into agreement with Jesus before He returns and releases His judgments. This is an aspect of the Great Commission that is often overlooked, but it is at the heart of the Great Commission. *The Great Commission will not be completed until the nations have been prepared for the return of Jesus.* Therefore, we must understand what is required to prepare the nations for Jesus.

## The Great Commission's Testimony to all Nations before the End Will Come

When it came time for God to deliver ancient Israel from Egypt, He sent Moses and Aaron as messengers to Egypt. They told Pharaoh what God wanted and instructed him to cooperate with God. Pharaoh refused, and God responded by releasing His judgments. When God's judgments came, Pharaoh was not confused about who was troubling Egypt or about what God wanted.

In the same way, God will not release His end-time judgments until the nations have been warned and instructed to cooperate with God:

*"And this gospel of the kingdom will be proclaimed throughout the whole world as a testimony to all nations, and then the end will come." (Matthew 24:14)*

Our mission is like the mission God gave Moses. We are to instruct the nations about God's coming deliverance and call the nations to cooperate with God's purposes.

The preaching of the gospel of the kingdom to all the nations is not just an offer of mercy to the nations, it is also a warning to the nations. The word *testimony* in Matthew 24:14 is the Greek word μαρτύριον (*marytrion*). This word was used to refer to a witness given by an individual who has firsthand evidence of a matter and, therefore, could serve as a legal witness to the truth in a court.

This means the messengers who fulfill Matthew 24:14 must have firsthand knowledge of the message, just as a witness has firsthand knowledge of an event. This requires an intimate relationship with Jesus and an intimate knowledge of the Scriptures. We must know Jesus and what He has said if we are going to prepare the nations for Him.

The gospel message is a witness given to the nations of what is true. When God judges the nations, they will be without excuse because they will have heard the proclamation of the church concerning what Jesus required. We can hardly imagine what it will be like when the nations stand before God for judgment without excuse because God sent witnesses to the nations before His end-time judgments.

Jesus ended Matthew 24:14 with the phrase *the end will come*. This phrase can also be translated as *God will finish everything*. The phrase *the end will come* refers to the events of the end of the age. This means the end of the age will not come until the witness of Matthew 24:14 is given in the nations. God is so merciful He will not allow the Antichrist to emerge in the earth until a warning has been given to all the nations about Jesus, His Kingdom, and His agenda.

## Matthew 24:14 and Matthew 24:15

Jesus shifted His teaching in Mathew 24:15 and began to reference specific end-time events the prophets had predicted. He said,

> *So when you see the abomination of desolation spoken of by the prophet Daniel, standing in the holy place (let the reader understand)....*

He began Matthew 24:15 with the word οὖν (*oun*) which is usually translated *so* or *therefore* (in the New American Standard Bible and the New King James Version). This word is a transition word that implies the conclusion of a thought that prepares for what follows. Jesus used this word to communicate Matthew 24:14 and Matthew 24:15 are directly connected. The events of Matthew 24:15 are the natural outcome of completing the witness to the nations, and Jesus wanted to make sure we understood preparing the nations for end-time events is part of what is required to fulfill Matthew 24:14.

In the same way that what comes before Matthew 24:4–13 is key to understanding Matthew 24:14, what comes after Matthew 24:15 is also key to understanding all that is included in the Matthew 24:14 witness. To fulfill Matthew 24:14, there must be a witness given that prepares the nations for everything that is involved in the abomination that Jesus refers to in verse 15. Therefore, to obey Jesus we must understand the abomination Daniel prophesied and all that is implicated in the abomination and associated with it.

It should be obvious in verse 15 that we must understand the abomination to prepare the nations for it, but the fact that we are specifically told to understand Daniel's prophecy means Jesus anticipated we would be tempted to overlook this. He knew we would be tempted to reduce Matthew 24:14 to evangelism and miss the requirement of preparing the nations for what is coming. *To obey Jesus, we must study the prophets, understand the main themes or what is coming, and then apply that to our missiology.*

We cannot fulfill Matthew 24:14 if we do not understand these things and give a witness to the nations about them. To say it another way, until the nations are prepared for what is implied by verse 15, the events of verse 15 will not happen. *Just as God did not release His judgments on Egypt until Pharaoh was warned, God is far too kind to allow the final hour of crisis to come on the earth before the nations have been given a witness.*

The nations must be warned, not only to repent of their sin, but also to not join a wicked man when he goes down to Jerusalem and leads the nations in a rage against Jesus by opposing God's plans for the city of Jerusalem and the Jewish people. We cannot understand the mission to every tribe and tongue without understanding the eschatological landscape in which the mission is completed. Our missiology must be the gospel of the kingdom, and it must prepare the earth for the abomination Jesus warned us is coming and a final siege on Jerusalem.

If our labor in the nations does not prepare the nations for what is coming, then it will come short of fulfilling Matthew 24:14. Only the full gospel of the kingdom that prepares the earth for God's end-time purposes can fulfill the ultimate mission of the Great Commission. This does not mean a simple message of evangelism is not important. It is critically important. It is the starting point for fulfilling Matthew 24:14. The nations must be presented the offer of salvation. It also does not mean every presentation of the gospel must include end-time details. It simply means nations must be warned and the church must be prepared in the process of discipling the nations.

Matthew 24:14 cannot be oversimplified to mean evangelization of the Gentiles will automatically result in Jesus' return. In God's mercy, He will not allow the end to come until the nations are ready to cooperate with His purposes for Jerusalem and for Israel. *The Great Commission is not finished until the church is prepared and the nations are warned.* This gives focus to the work of missions. It must begin with evangelism, but it also must disciple nations for what is coming. If our missions work does not achieve this objective, it has not yet fulfilled Matthew 24:14, regardless of the regions reached.

When we view Matthew 24:14 in context, we can summarize the Great Commission as a threefold task:

1. Expand the church by evangelism.

2. Prepare the church for the return of Jesus and all that it entails through understanding God's plan.

3. Warn the nations to cooperate with God's end-time purposes.

## The Great Commission—More than Evangelism

Part of understanding God's plan for Israel and the nations is understanding how the Great Commission prepares the nations for the conclusion of God's plan. We must understand how the age ends so we can prepare the church for it. We must understand God's plan to save the nations, His plan to save Israel, and how He has joined the two together.

We are used to thinking of the Great Commission only as evangelism and only as something that affects the Gentile nations. Evangelism is the beginning of the Great Commission, but it goes much further than that. We are preparing the nations for a glorious plan in which the salvation of Israel and the salvation of the nations are inseparably joined. The Great Commission sets the context for that to happen.

We must restore the connection between Israel and the great Commission. The two are not at odds. God loves Israel *and* the nations. He has purposes for Israel *and* the Gentiles. He will fulfill His promises by joining both together in deep relationship—in one family—under His Son Jesus. In this family, Israel and the Gentiles will each play a specific role, and we want to play our specific role for the sake of the entire family.

*Our task, and our joy, is to disciple the nations with the understanding of the glory of God's plan so we can labor with Him for the fulfillment of all He has promised.*

Samuel Whitefield's primary labor is as an intercessor in the context of night and day prayer. He is also an author and speaker. He is the director of OneKing, a ministry that helps connect the global church to God's purposes for Israel and the nations. He also serves on the senior leadership team of the International House of Prayer of Kansas City and as faculty at the International House of Prayer University.

For additional resources please visit samuelwhitefield.com.

Made in the USA
Columbia, SC
28 November 2018